The Incredible
PRESENCE OF JESUS

By IRene Hamm

This book is dedicated to all the courageous men and women who came to Rising Above, a faith-based treatment center.

YOU ARE MY HEROES

The Lord bless you, and keep you;
The Lord make His face shine on you,
and be gracious to you;
the Lord lift up His countenance on you,
- and give you peace.

– Numbers 6:24-26

The Incredible Presence of Jesus
By IRene Hamm

Edited by Linda Wasylciw.
Front and back cover by Irene Hamm
Photo by Irene Hamm

Table of Contents

Introduction

Someone absolutely adores you, and His love is unconditional. Not only does He delight in you, but He has been with you from the moment you were conceived, and will continue to be with you until your last breath. In His presence, pain transforms into peace, sorrow is replaced with joy; guilt, anger, and shame are released. This reality is written in this book; the Incredible Presence of Jesus. It is yours to experience.

Throughout history, God made it known that He longs to be near us. Before Jesus left this earth, He told us to be sure of one thing: He will be with us always, even to the ends of the age.[1] Come into the presence of Jesus. He will fill your heart, overflowing it with His love and His peace. He invites you.

John 7:37-38 - Jesus stood and shouted to the crowds, "Anyone who is thirsty may come to me! Anyone who believes in Me may come and drink!" For the Scriptures declare, 'Rivers of living water will flow from his heart.'

Within this book, I have intertwined God's written word with what I have experienced. Together, they create powerful evidence that Jesus truly is with us – always, and He deeply loves us. Biblical truth is the foundation on which experiences rest. Experiencing Jesus, sweetens God's truth.

Milton wrote: 'From the evidence of divine revelation, we must add recorded human experience. Experience by itself is an unreliable witness. . .But when Scripturally-validated experience - case studies, and reports, . . . is

---

[1] Matthew 28:20

1

coupled with the testimony of the Holy Bible, we have the most reliable case study from which to gather facts.'[2]

Among the many Scripture verses, I have written of my own experiences with Jesus, and what I have witnessed. Permission has been granted for me to write about various people's experiences during their Inner Healing Sessions. The names of the people involved may have been changed. Every encounter was glorious, because of Jesus' presence and the truth He spoke.

Our souls crave love, acceptance, and belonging to someone. Our hearts long for warmth, comfort, and rejuvenation. Be assured, an encounter with Jesus is waiting for you. Discover healing of woundedness through the Presence of Jesus. It is possible to be free from anger, guilt, and shame. Let Him touch your soul with His words of truth. He is inviting you into His Presence.

Over the years in which I have facilitated Inner Healing Sessions, I have come alongside others as they followed their emotions to the memory where their painful beliefs began. They discovered that Jesus was present. When Jesus spoke, by way of thought or pictures, they knew His words were true and healing flowed deeply into their souls. Transformation happened. Their painful beliefs were replaced with a peaceful knowing of the truth. Chaotic pain transformed into tranquil peacefulness. Their memory no longer held its sting.

Enter Jesus' Presence. He delights in you, rejoicing over you with joyful songs.[3] In His Presence, you are loved, accepted, and belong. Your soul is free to soar. Jesus beckons you into His presence. His arms are open wide, eager to receive you into His embrace, bringing satisfaction into the depths of your soul. Come to the Healer.

---

[2] Dr. Michael A. Milton, Are Demons Real and What Power Do They Have Today? Jan.29, 2019, http://www.biblestudytools.com
[3] Zephaniah 3:17

John 6:35- Jesus replied, "I am the Bread of Life. Whoever comes to me will never be hungry again. Whoever believes in me will never be thirsty."

Perhaps, your only connection with Jesus is wearing a cross, as a necklace. Or maybe, you have been told about Jesus, yet you do not sense Him nor hear Him. Knowing of Jesus, yet not experiencing Him, cannot satisfy one's hungry soul. But if you have experienced the presence of Jesus, a cross on a necklace is a powerful symbol of His death and resurrection. That piece of jewelry reminds you of His amazing presence in your life. When the presence of Jesus is experienced, His fullness infiltrates your inner being.

I cannot remain silent when souls are crying out for healing. Jesus longs to touch us. It is true - Jesus loves us dearly and is able to heal emotional pain. He understands our pain and, when we invite Him, He touches our woundedness. Healing happens. Come with me, open your heart and soul to Jesus.

At the end of every chapter, I have allowed space for you to write in response to the written questions. Take time to think of each topic and apply it to your own life. Experience His Presence, His healing.

I invite you to come with me as I share God's Word and my reflections of experiencing the Presence of Jesus. Encountering the living Lord is incredible, beyond all possible imaginations. Jesus' presence will not disappoint, for He will touch the depth of your being with ultimate satisfaction. Come. Jesus invites you. Taste the deeply satisfying and thrilling goodness of God.

Taste and see that the Lord is good.
Oh, the joys of those
who take refuge in Him.
- Psalm 34:8

REFLECTIONS: Introduction

1. What do you long for in life?
2. What are some things you have done to fulfil that longing?
3. What is your experience regarding God/Jesus?
4. For which of your wounds do you desire healing?
5. Come to Jesus with your open heart.
   He is the amazing Healer

Notes & Journaling:

PART 1

Grasping Reality

Imagination opens the door
to the reality of Jesus' presence.

Jesus is the Son of God.
He is the visible image of God.
We can know Him, His voice.

Though life is not understandable,
God's character is trustworthy.

Chapter 1

Jesus and Imagination

When my son was in high school, he purchased a ball python. The snake was small, non-threatening. But in a few years, it grew to 39 inches or 100 centimeters in length.

One day the snake slithered out of its aquarium and by the time we noticed its absence, it could have been anywhere within the house. My husband refused to sleep in our bedroom and he headed to the upper room of our barn. I went to bed alone. At 2:30 a.m., I awoke to see a dark curve on the pillow beside me. There lay the snake, staring at me with its beady eyes.

I called upon my daughter, who promptly put it back where it belonged, then I fell asleep. But in the morning, I struggled to remain focused. I had visions of the snake coming up my leg while in bed, twisting and slithering from my ankles to my thighs. It was a slow torturous advance creating terror.

Imagine such a situation happening to you. You may feel dread, fear, shivers, or maybe some chuckles. Emotions radiate when imagination has been activated. Your mind has the ability to experience situations.

2 Corinthians 10:5 suggests that we have the ability to take every thought captive. So, I plugged my mind's ears and eyes of the taunting reality of what had happened, and focused on my mind's song of 'la la la'. I stopped those thoughts from torturing me. It was incredible that I had authority over the mocking voice of terror within my being. My mind became quiet.

Imagination is very powerful. It can:
- take you to any place.
- place you in the company of anyone.
- accomplish anything.
- re-write the past.
- affect the future.

Imagination's flexible nature morphs to support our perspective of situations. It creates beliefs that feel true. Imagination is creative and takes residence within our thinking.

When we worry, we imagine something dreadful, making us feel overwhelmed. Our thoughts are continuously moving, re-imagining what did happen or what could have happened. When we anticipate a thrilling event, we imagine it with joy, endorphins flow throughout our beings. Sometimes imagination creates our fantasy, fulfilling a void, a longing within us for desirable circumstances. At times, imagination enables us to escape a painful or disappointing reality.

We create thoughts within our mind throughout the day. Continuously. We dwell on it or let it go. We have control of our imagination.

Our imagination and thoughts are constantly creating situations within our minds. Weighing. Evaluating. Concluding. Wishing. Dreading. Hoping. Imagination is something that we have not experienced – yet – and may never. Our thoughts and feelings have lined up to produce a supposed reality.

What about the reality of Jesus' presence? In Matthew 28:20, Jesus announced: "Be sure of this, I am with you always – even to the end of the age."

There is no exception to 'always'. Whether I was experiencing the joy of a new grandchild or the intense sorrow of my daughter's death, He was with me.

He was the One who knit us together in our mother's womb.[4] No matter where we go, we can never get away from His presence.[5] He is *always* with us.

Throughout this book, I mention the presence of Jesus - the reality of His Presence. Sensing Jesus in a memory is not imagination; His presence is sensed. It is real.

When I met with people in the Inner Healing Sessions, their raw wounds were exposed for our Healer, Jesus, to touch. It was a privilege to walk with them into the awareness of Jesus. While in the pain of their memory, I asked – "Where are you Jesus?" Sometimes His presence was sensed but often it was 'seen', within the memory. Sensing or seeing Jesus is not imagination. He says that He is with us – ALWAYS. I have sensed Him when my heart was crying; I have observed other people 'see' Him during an Inner Healing Session. I am witness to His reality.

- Can imaginations be used by God? Absolutely.
- Can imaginations be used by Satan? Absolutely. God destroyed the earth in Noah's time because every thought and imagination was evil.[6]

2 Corinthians 10:4-5 states that any speculation or imagination that is against the knowledge of God, is to be cast down. Therefore, any imagination that does not agree with what God says or who He is, is not from God. Think about pornography: it is visual, physical and stimulating, activating the imagination. It takes over one's thinking and controls emotions. This imagination is not pleasing to God.

But when we imagine Jesus' presence with us, our imagination is in line with what is true and good. We never are alone.

---

[4] Psalm 139:13
[5] Psalm 139:7
[6] Genesis 6:5

He has been and is with us - always.

- He understands us.
- He feels our woes.
- His eyes overflow with compassion.
- Strength flows into our being.
- His love consumes our souls.

Our hearts thirst for love from His eyes. When we hear His voice, life flows into our being, fills us with peace – a deep peace down in the depth of our souls. He sets us free to live when He heals us.

When I 'hear' God, He speaks to me in my thoughts. Sometimes they are powerful revelations of truth and, at times, they are a gentleness that stills my soul. I often see pictures in my mind. These communications reflect the character of God.

Like any relationship, it takes time to recognize the voice of Jesus. If a stranger phoned me, I would not recognize her voice. But if she phoned every day, I would soon be able to identify her. Jesus speaks of sheep recognizing the voice of their shepherd.[7] When sheep are in their shepherd's presence, they know his voice. Even in the dark, they know who he is. It is the same in knowing the voice of our Shepherd, Jesus. Demons know that Jesus is God's Son, but He is not their Shepherd; they do not have a relationship with Him. Relationship is about interacting with Him, experiencing Him. The Shepherd's heart touches my soul, my knowing and believing.

God the Father highly esteemed His Son, Jesus. As I uplift Jesus, I am engaging in the Father's exaltation of Him. God has elevated Jesus to the place of highest honour and someday, every knee will bow down before Him, every tongue will confess Jesus as Lord to the glory of God, the Father.[8] When

---

[7] John 10:3-5
[8] Philippians 2:9-11

we worship Jesus, we join Father God and Spirit God in exalting the Son of God, Jesus. That is what God wants us to do – bring blessing, honour, glory, and power to Jesus.

I write this book to honour Jesus. He is the Son of God, the One who saved us. He alone is our Healer. Because of His suffering and His death, our wounds are healed. We identify with Jesus. He was God, in human form.

Hebrews 2:14 – Because God's children are human beings – made of flesh and blood – the Son also became flesh and blood.

Thousands of people observed Jesus during his life on Earth. For thirty-three years, the people interacted with Jesus. They were beholding God. He was the visible image of the invisible God.[9] People touched Him and He responded in kind. Men and women listened to His voice and He attended to them. They saw Jesus walking from village to village; His feet made footprints in the dirt. He became hungry. He was angry. He loved the children. He spoke to women and those rejected as despicable. He touched those who had leprosy and He touched the eyes of those who could not see. He saw men sitting in trees and those bound in chains. He went to those who were crying in the darkness, the broken-hearted. His heart was evident; it revealed the heart of His Father, God.

The Bible reveals who God is, by what Jesus said and how He acted. The character of God is exposed. We can understand what God loves and what makes Him sad. We can learn what pleases Him and what is disrespectful to Him. Our society and culture today are different than it was in Jesus' day, and yet, when we know the heart of God; we know what pleases Him.

---

[9] Colossians 1:15

My daughter died nearly two years ago, at the time of this writing. In present situations, I have imagined what she would have said, in her wittiness, or how she would have reacted to various situations. Because I knew her character, I can accurately predict how she would have reacted in my present situations. Just so, as I know Jesus, I can know His words and responses because I know His character, His heart.

Since Jesus is the visible image of God, that is who we identify with. No one has seen Father God and few have seen the Holy Spirit. At Pentecost, the Spirit came upon the believers as tongues of fire,[10] and at Jesus' baptism, the Spirit came down like a dove.[11] But rarely was He seen. In John 3, the Holy Spirit is compared to the wind.[12] We cannot see wind, but we are aware of its effects on us. The Spirit of God interacts with us, but it is Jesus who we identify with. Imagination allows us to 'see' Jesus within our memory. It is Jesus whom we identify with.

I have led hundreds of Inner Healing Sessions over the years and witnessed the effects of Jesus' presence and His words. His presence was not an imagination but a reality. It:

- disposed of the heavy burdens of guilt.
- plucked off shame.
- replaced anger with peace.
- forgave the unforgivable.
- soothed sorrow.
- dissipated sadness.
- spoke liberating truth.
- filled their being with life – purpose – peace.

At the beginning of each session, I spoke a prayer, acknowledging Jesus' Presence, asking Him to direct me as

---

[10] Acts 2:3
[11] John 1:32
[12] John 3:8

facilitator. I trusted Him to open the way of healing for the troubled individual. I sensed Him standing among us. I knew it was Jesus, the Healer, bringing peace.

During the Inner Healing Session, the person sensed the presence of Jesus within their painful memory. Jesus spoke truth to them and they knew He loved them deeply. Peace flowed. He was present; they were not alone.

I invite you to be aware of Jesus' presence. Be still. Look around. He is present. Imagination opens the door to sense Him in our memories of the past and into our present world. But, sensing His presence goes far beyond our imagination, for there is a new knowing of truth. It heals our wounds.

There are many ways that we can experience Jesus:
- in nature; the creation of God
- through music or another person's words
- through a dream or a vision
- through an angel or supernatural occurrence
- most commonly, by way of a gentle voice within our minds

I experience deep peace when I envision Jesus with me, and with others. I invite His presence to be near. It is powerful and breathes life.

JESUS IN THE CAR:
Several years ago, my husband was driving back to Alberta from British Columbia, through the beautiful Rocky Mountains. It was October and the roads were very slippery. I was at home, imagining the icy roads, dreading what could transpire. Suddenly, I had a strange, heavy feeling. Something dreadful was going to happen. Fear overtook me.

15

Then I remembered that Jesus was with us all the time. I closed my eyes and looked for Jesus in my husband's car. And there He was. I saw Him in my mind. He was sitting in the passenger seat. His shoulder length hair was blowing back. I sensed that He was full of joy as He hung onto the dashboard, ready and excited for action. I felt God's deep peace flow over me. I knew that my husband was going to be okay. Jesus was with him.

About half an hour later, my husband phoned me, but there was not enough time for him to tell me his story. Something had happened, I did not know what. Yet, God's peace continued to flow into my soul. Jesus was with him, and my husband was alive. An hour later my husband phoned again and told me what had happened. The car had been swerving from side to side then instead of rolling, the car went flying off the road, through the air; like a jet taking off. (I realized why Jesus was hanging onto the dashboard.) The car landed thirty feet down the ravine, up against the trees. My husband managed to get out of the car and crawled on his hands and knees, up the incline, back to the road.

I felt such a tranquil peace knowing that Jesus was right there with my husband. There were many possible outcomes with terrible endings, but my husband was talking to me. He was alive and he was okay. Jesus was with him.

Have you ever experienced the presence of Jesus? He has always been with you, is with you today, and will be with you for all your tomorrows. You are breathing today because God has purpose in you being alive. Allow His presence into your life, He longs to be welcomed, to be close beside you.

PRAYER:

Dear Jesus. I didn't know that You have been with me every day of my life. I didn't know that I have never been alone. I really need You! I need You to hold me and speak to me. I open my heart and mind to You. I ask You to come close beside me. In Jesus' name, Amen.

BE SURE OF THIS: I AM WITH YOU ALWAYS, EVEN TO THE END OF THE AGE.
Matthew 28:20

REFLECTIONS: Chapter 1 – Jesus and Imagination

1. What does your imagination dwell on?
2. How can you take your imagination captive, under your control?
3. When have you sensed the presence of Jesus? How did it make you feel?
4. What does it feel like to know that Jesus has always been with you, is with you now, and is always going to be with you in your future?

Notes & Journaling:

_____

_____

_____

_____

_____

_____

_____

_____

_____

_____

_____

_____

Chapter 2

Jesus is Trustworthy

Over the last few months, she was more concerned with her hair, her makeup, her matching shoes. She became protective of her phone, guarding it. She went on business trips. She spoke of these ventures as important, necessary for the advancement of the company. Red flags waved – at first subtly, then more intensely. One day, the truth was exposed. She was seeing someone else – her boss. Trust shattered into a million pieces. The pain cut deep into the depth of her husband's soul.

Trust is a confident expectation of someone, an assured hope, a knowing. We have all experienced betrayal in our lifetime. Broken trust shatters our confidence. Once broken, trust must be earned, bit by bit.

It may feel like God is not trustworthy; He seems unreliable. Trust is severed when our expectations have not been met. It is human that we struggle to understand His ways. There may be times when it does not feel that He is anywhere around, nor that He cares. Our souls cry out, demanding answers. We ask ourselves, 'Is He trustworthy?'

Exodus 34:6 states that God is compassionate, merciful, patient, slow to anger and filled with unfailing love and faithfulness.[13] These characteristics are ones that we crave to have in someone we trust.

Three statements that God declares about Himself:

- He is all-loving.
- He is all-powerful.

---

[13] Exodus 34:6

- He is all-knowing.

At times, we may wonder how a loving and powerful God, who knows everything, can allow brutality to happen within our world. Sometimes cruelty is the result of choices – what is said or done. God gave free will to all mankind. Yet our choices do not determine God's character – He is still all-loving, all-powerful and all-knowing, no matter what choices we make. He is present. He is with us as life brings both joy and pain.

Some life events are explainable. But, at times, there seems to be no explanation. Life's happenings feel harsh, ruthless, and inexcusable.

GONE IN A HEARTBEAT:

My husband's cousin was doing what he did every day - driving truck, hauling stuff. No one knew this would be his last day alive on earth.

That October day, he was driving through the mountains, just like many previous days, twisting through the magnificent, humungous mounds of rock, along with all the other cars and trucks. But a large boulder loosened from its perch, on the mountainside. It began to move. Its descent accelerated. Gravity compelled its downward plunge, urging it with increasing dominance, squarely hitting the truck's roof. His last breath escaped his lips. His heartbeat ceased. His life ended.

God says that His Word holds true and we can trust everything He does.[14] Proverbs states that we are to trust God with all our heart and not lean on our own understanding.[15] He is God. Isaiah 55:8-9 declares that His thoughts are not our thoughts and His ways are not our ways. We are not able to comprehend His thoughts nor what He does. His plans are a totally different level, majestic and powerful.

---

[14] Psalm 33:4
[15] Proverbs 3:5

20

Ecclesiastes 11:5 – Just as you cannot understand the path of the wind or the mystery of a tiny baby growing in its mother's womb, so you cannot understand the activity of God, who does all things.

Just because we cannot understand the ways of God, does not mean that He is not trustworthy.

Jesus stated that we would have many trials and sorrows on Earth.[16] He did not promise leisurely strolls in the park, with the warm sun shining every day, of birds singing amidst a gentle breeze. He said that we should not be surprised when threatening events occur. They are to be expected.

Trust and faith are intertwined. When we believe and move in faith, God reveals His trustworthiness. Hebrews 11 begins with miraculous happenings by God's hands. Due to faith, kingdoms were overthrown, justice ruled and promises were fulfilled. Lions' mouths were shut. Flames of fire were quenched. Death was conquered. Whole armies were put into flight and women received their loved ones spared from death. Then the consequences of faith changed. God's people, unwilling to deny their Jesus, were tortured, jeered at, their backs cut with whips. They were chained and imprisoned. Stoned. Sawn in half. Killed by sword. Destitute and oppressed. Mistreated. Their faith assured them that He was trustworthy, even though He had not yet provided what He had promised them.

Romans 8:35,37-38 - Does it mean God no longer loves us if we have trouble or calamity, or are persecuted, or hungry or destitute, or in danger, or threatened with death? . . . No, despite all these things, overwhelming victory is ours through Christ, who loved us. And I am convinced that nothing can ever separate us from God's love.

---

[16] John 16:33

Life is sometimes emotionally overwhelming. Every one of us have challenges and struggles. Some battles are hidden from view while others are visible to those around us. Everyone of us have challenges, no one is exempt. Jesus said difficulties would come in life. He stated that we would experience hardship, sometimes excruciating hard times.

Pain is a part of life. At times, we feel frozen within our struggles and unable to proceed, trapped with no visible exit. We may feel victimized, angry and helpless, with no control over what life has dealt us. We cry out, asking God why this happened. Our sense of love and justice concludes that if we keep the golden rule, we will be blessed. Many people believe in karma: whatever you have done or not done you reap the consequences accordingly. Galatians 6:7 states we will harvest what we plant. The consequences of our actions and /or words are always present, and yet, sometimes life goes contrary to what we should have earned.

JOB'S STORY:

In the Biblical story of Job, he tried to understand the tragedies in his life, but could not. Everything he had once experienced with God, did not fit with what had just taken place in his life.

Job was a man who had integrity, not only in his own eyes but in God's eyes as well.[17] Job was the richest man in the land of Uz with many sheep, camels, teams of oxen, female donkeys, plus servants. His family consisted of seven sons, three daughters and his wife. In the Old Testament, God pronounced that a good person would be blessed, and yet, in one day, Job lost everything.

Later that day, Job received the news that the wind had collapsed the house in which all his sons and daughters had been partying. All of his beloved children died. All ten of them.

---

[17] Job 1:8

22

His soul was overwhelmed. Nothing made sense. He wondered – 'What is God doing?'

It got worse. Job's skin erupted with boils, covering his entire being. Large oozing pockets of pus covered his body from head to toe. He sat on the ground, scraping his skin with a shattered piece of pottery. His body screamed in pain; He had no place of comfort. His wife mocked him for believing in God, and told him to curse God. His close friends accused Job of being guilty, that he must have deserved this destruction. But Job knew he was blameless, therefore, it did not make sense that God would cause all this destruction upon him.

Why do bad things happen to good people? There may never be a visible nor satisfying answer. Perhaps a better question to ask is this: "What am I going to do now?"

Job had to face his devastation. He searched within himself, trying to make sense of what life had dealt him. He knew that he was innocent. He cursed the day that he was born, yet he hung onto his God, who permitted such pain and devastation. Job could not understand God's ways and His thoughts, yet He knew God's character. Before this devastation happened, he knew that God was good, so Job fell down before God and worshipped Him for who He was.[18]

MY STORY:

My second child, Cherie, was born with malformed eyes resulting in blindness. My husband and I had no idea that anything was wrong with our baby, until she was born. A mass of scar tissue, inside each of her eyes, had inhibited them from developing normally, when she was within my womb. After birth, Cherie was tested for the most common viruses that could have caused the eye damage. No cause was discovered. Genetic testing was done, revealing no answers. We asked the

---

[18] Job 1:20

23

question "Why?" and received no answers. So, we asked a new question, "What are we going to do now?"

Having a blind daughter shattered my world. All my dreams and expectations for my little girl exploded. So many broken pieces. When she was seven months old, we were told that she had cerebral palsy. As she grew, she needed the assistance of a walker. I felt totally unequipped to mother my daughter, who had such huge challenges.

One afternoon, when Cherie was just over two years old, I sensed God asking me, in my mind, if I would allow Him to do whatever He wanted with Cherie. The memory is very clear; I can still envision the steel divider on the bathroom window as I was washing it. Time stood still. I stopped what I was doing. God's question took me by surprise.

What was He asking of me? I did not answer Him right away – I could not. I loved my daughter. I asked myself. 'Is God trustworthy? Is He good?'

I had three options:
1. I could totally reject God. He had allowed all sorts of suffering and pain in my daughter's life already. Was He dependable? Was He planning more hardships for her? I could reject God, send Him out of my life. But I realized that I could not remove Him, I needed Him. He was my stability. I poured out my heart to Him and He held me, wiped away my tears. He was my strength and my refuge. No, I could not reject Him.
2. The second option was to keep my relationship with Him but not trust Him all the time. I would trust Him sometimes, then other times, I would take control. But that was not a realistic choice. That choice would bring confusion and chaos into my life. Either He was trustworthy or He was not. My emotions and logic must agree. No, that was not a reasonable choice at all.

24

3. The third option was to commit to trusting Him completely, 100%, with no hesitation. That was the only way to have absolute peace. I also realized that whether I chose to trust Him or not, I still had to deal with the challenges that life brought me. I needed Him as my Cheerleader, my Sustainer, Giver of joy and strength. I decided to trust Him. Completely. With no conditions. No swaying or deviation.

I WILL TRUST YOU, OH GOD.

Psalm 46:10 :
    BE still and know that I am God.
    Be **STILL** and know that I am God.
    Be still **AND** know that I am God.
    Be still and **KNOW** that I am God.
    Be still and know **THAT** I am God.
    Be still and know that **I** am God.
    Be still and know that I **AM** God.
    Be still and know that I am **GOD**.

My trust became unshakeable. Firm. Resolute. No matter how difficult life was, I chose to believe:
- God was trustworthy. His words are truth.
- He deeply loved me and was with me.

God has proven Himself to be trustworthy, even when I could not understand the 'why'. Trusting in Him was the best choice I could have made. God upheld me when I was weary and gave me wisdom when I was overwhelmed. He was my Strength.

Isaiah 40:31 – But those who trust in the Lord will find new strength. They will soar high on wings like eagles. They will run and not grow weary. They will walk and not faint.

My journey of trust began at age eleven when I invited Jesus into my life. I repented of my sin, and I received His forgiveness. I talked to Him often. My relationship with Him slowly evolved, drinking in His presence, His love. I listened to Him. I knew that He loved me in spite of my human flaws. I knew that He was with me.

I learned to anchor myself in Jesus. I talked with Him and chose to trust Him. Trust was an action that strengthened my faith like a muscle. Exercising trust in the little things, preparing me for life's bigger challenges. He was the only One to completely trust. I drew near to Him, so that I could look into His eyes and receive His love. His love was delightful.

When I made the choice to trust Him, He filled me with joy. Though I cannot always understand Him, He is faithful. His character never changes. He does not disappoint me. Jesus is trustworthy.

PRAYER:
Dear God, it is scary to trust in You. But there is nothing else to trust in. I can't even trust myself. So, I choose to trust in You. I need you. Give me strength to keep looking at You. Fill me with Your peace. In Jesus name, Amen.

For I know the One in whom I trust,

and I am sure that He is able to guard what

I have entrusted to Him

until the day of His return.

- II Timothy 1:12

REFLECTIONS: Chapter 2 – Jesus is Trustworthy

1. What strengthens your trust with Jesus?
2. Discuss the 3 statements about God: He is loving; He is all-knowing; He is all-powerful.
3. Why would people be disappointed in God?
4. How does free will (your choice) affect what God does or does not do?
5. What does it look like, when you lean on your understanding instead of trusting Him?
6. What does trust have to do with faith?
7. Discuss Job's devastation and his response to God. What is your response when life seems unfair?
8. Which option, in trusting God, is the most common for you?
9. What are you trusting God for right now? What does it
10. look like to trust Him? Write down your commitment to trust in Him.

Notes & Journaling:

_____
_____
_____
_____
_____
_____
_____
_____
_____
_____
_____
_____
_____
_____

PART 2

God's Heart

God has always longed
to be with us.
It is mankind who determines
how close He comes.

God gave us choice,
therefore,
He pre-planned reconciliation.

It is possible to come close.
God's holiness and our sinful state
are able to co-exist - because of Jesus.

Chapter 3

The Story of Love

I have a son. He is not just an ordinary son. He was expelled from school and school districts. People gave up on him. They wondered how I could love a boy such as him. He was disruptive. He did things that made people shake their heads. He stirred up anger within others. He was seen as a wreck of a boy, one that caused wreckage.

At age fifteen, he was kicked out of his adoptive home. His eyes were full of sorrow; he did not feel like he belonged anywhere. His history of neglect caused him to feel unloved and thrown away. He had experienced numerous foster homes, one of them kept him for only one day. He was too much to handle. It seemed like nobody loved him. Nobody saw his broken heart. He felt rejected; he was rejected.

His wounds were a festering mess, and he had nowhere to go. That was when he came to our door and became part of my family. I grew to love this teenager. I saw his wounded heart. I embraced him. He became my son. My gift.

As an adult, he made destructive choices. I visited him in his crack house because I loved him. There were months when I did not hear from him. When someone told me they had seen him, I thanked God that my son was alive. I loved him.

My son spent time in jail. We talked on the phone and I visited him. I touched him and hugged him. I was his mom; he was my son.

After his release from jail, he had a partner, then a child — a little baby girl. Several years later, a son. They are my grandchildren and they delight me. They are in my heart, along with the rest of my family. I deeply love each of them.

I John 4:16 - God is love.

God's love is tender, powerful, and unconditional. He has always loved us, never turning away. His love is forever, unfailing.

From the beginning of time, God's deep desire was to fully express His love. It could not be contained. With powerful words, His creativity burst from His being for six days, expressing His imagination. And it became. It gave Him great pleasure. The heavens sang; the Earth exalted Him.

Psalm 19:1-4 - The heavens proclaim the glory of God. The skies display His craftsmanship. Day after day they continue to speak; night after night they make Him known. They speak without a sound or word; Their voice is never heard. Yet their message has gone throughout the Earth, and their words to all the world.

Creation is stunning. Consider the sunrise and sunset. Sometimes they are obscured with a thick blanket of clouds; sometimes they are magnificent. The whole world observes this magnificent drama unfold every day. See the hues of colour within this world – every tint is represented within its contours. Think about the spectacular solar systems, light years apart – massive, expanding beyond time, never ending. Then, there are the molecular systems of the human body – complex, precisely defined. Our Creator is amazing.

Of all creation brought forth into existence, the last was His treasured creation. His hands took the dirt of the ground and cleverly formed it. Every intricate part was designed with purpose, shaped from the earth. God breathed the breath of life into man. It was the very breath that had spoken all else into existence. The man was no longer dust of the earth, but a living being. God gave him a name, Adam. In God's wisdom,

He complemented the makeup of the man by creating a companion, a woman. She was given a name, Eve. These amazing creations were made in the image of God.

James 1:18 – We, out of all creation, became His prized possession.

God walked with them in the splendid garden. Without inhibitions, they communed as intimate friends and openly shared their hearts. They had no weakness nor apprehension, no fear nor shame – only acceptance and belonging in the presence of love. They experienced intense pleasure and satisfaction, longing for nothing. Their entire beings – their minds, hearts, bodies and spirits functioned perfectly, exactly according to their created purpose.

God, in His deep love, created Adam and Eve with free will, the ability to reason and make choices. In every situation, there is choice with the possibility of making the wrong selection. Without choice, we would be robots, programed and dictated by our Creator.

One day, Adam and Eve were in the garden admiring a tree laden with fruit. It was not an ordinary tree. That tree held their destiny. There was power in the tree, the power to choose. God had told them not to eat of its fruit; it was forbidden. But, the beauty of the fruit drew them.

The serpent slyly convinced Eve and Adam that the One who claimed to love them, was actually keeping goodness from them. "Go ahead, eat the fruit," the serpent enticed them.

Deception twisted and obscured the truth, undermining it. Deception wanted to control. The temptation seduced and overtook them; the lies became appealing. Adam and Eve made the choice to fulfil their own desires. They took the forbidden fruit and ate it.

Disobedience happened. Their cravings led to sinful actions which in turn opened the door to death.[19] Sin was birthed into existence.

Romans 5:12 – When Adam sinned, sin entered the world. Adam's sin brought death, so death spread to everyone, for everyone sinned.

God entered the garden to walk with them, but Adam and Eve were hiding, ashamed of what they had done. Sin does that. It drags us away from God's presence. It obscures His presence from our eyes. Adam and Eve stayed out of God's sight. They tried to escape the presence of the One who deeply loved them. But they could not hide, God was aware of everything. They could not hide from His eyes. He knew they had sinned.

Adam and Eve were afraid to face their Father, their Creator, whom they had disobeyed.
- Afraid of rejection.
- Afraid of the wages of death they had just earned.
- Afraid that this was the end of their beautiful love story.

Because they had chosen to make up their own rules, the fragrant presence of love was overtaken by the searing pain of rejection. Separation happened.

But love did not give up. It cannot. Love is patient; it is kind. Love is unconditional. It does not ignore nor does it walk away. It perseveres.[20] God longed to be with them. He asked Adam, "Where are you?"[21] His heart was yearning to be with them, to spend time with them.

God mercifully gave Adam and Eve the opportunity to own their sin, to repent. He longed for them to confess their rebellious act so He could forgive them. Instead, Adam blamed

---

[19] James 1:14-15
[20] 1 Corinthians 13:4-7
[21] Genesis 3:9

Eve, and Eve blamed the serpent and the deceptive serpent knew he had won. Sin had entered the world and become their master.

Adam and Eve carried incredible guilt, like a millstone chained to their throat. The One whom they adored was now the One they could not face. The shame – it suffocated the vibrancy of life as a heavy coat of ugliness. Unclean. Unacceptable. Undone.

God, in His mercy, made coverings for them out of animal skins,[22] the first sacrifice given on behalf of sin. The presence of murderous death had never occurred before. Its sting was piercing. It caused havoc in the continuation of life. It was fatal. They watched as death robbed the animal of life. The blood of this animal spilled on the ground, as a result of their disobedience. Adam and Eve were the guilty ones - not the animal. A loved creature had to die, to pay for their disobedience, to cover their shame. Their sinful state was cloaked in animal skins.

God removed them from the garden. They had to leave their paradise, the place that filled them with joy and utterly satisfied their souls. Imagine the intense grief that God, Adam and Eve felt when their sweet communion was severed. I know that feeling. I was present when my daughter died and left me behind on this earth. Separation from the one you love causes excruciating agony.

Adam and Eve were expelled from the garden. But God did not leave them. He did not reject them. He did not turn His back on them nor disown them. He was still their Father and they were His children – His beloved children. God remained present. He loved. He forgave.

Throughout the Old Testament, God continuously interacted with His people in all sorts of ways.[23] He spoke

---

[22] Genesis. 3:21
[23] Hebrews 1:1

through His written Word or directly to them, sometimes through dreams or nature, at times through angels and His prophets. On one occasion He used a donkey.[24] He communicated by writing on the wall.[25] God was not limited in how He spoke to mankind; it was mankind's reception that limited Him from being heard.

GOD WITH HIS PEOPLE

ENOCH:
There was a man named Enoch who had a close relationship with God. He was so close to God that one day he disappeared – gone, no longer on this earth, for God had taken Enoch to Himself,[26] out of love.

NOAH:
Noah, in his day, was the only one who listened to God. Everyone else disobeyed Him. They made up their own directions of life. But Noah was different. He revered God. Whatever God told him to do, he did it - even if the instructions were ridiculous. Noah did not follow his own reasoning. When told to build an ark, he followed God's instructions. It took him decades. He obeyed even though everyone mocked him; they thought he was crazy. But then it happened. It rained continuously for forty days and nights; the earth flooded. Everything died except for Noah, his family and the animals he had taken into the ark. They were saved because he obeyed God. God created the rainbow to remind mankind that He would not destroy the earth again.[27]

Proverbs 3:5 – Trust in the Lord with all your heart; do not depend on your own understanding.

---

[24] Numbers 22:28-30
[25] Daniel 5:5
[26] Genesis 5:23
[27] Genesis 9:12-17

ABRAHAM:

Abraham and God had many conversations, some of them were through angels, God's messengers. God declared that Abraham's descendants would be His chosen people.[28] Even though both Abraham and his wife were exceptionally old, the angels told them they were going to have a son, Isaac, from whom a huge nation would be birthed. God declared that the descendants would be as numerous as the stars in the sky. It was a promise that God kept, blessing them as His people.

Psalm 33:4 – The Word of God holds true and we can trust everything He does.

JACOB:

Jacob wrestled with a man, a mortal who was God Himself.[29] They scrimmaged all night. Jacob asked the man his name but received no answer. Jacob realized he was seeing God, face to face. And although they fought, his life was spared. Jacob asked God to bless him. God changed Jacob's name to Israel and he fathered twelve sons who became the twelve tribes of Israel.

I Chronicles 4:10 – "Oh, that You would bless me in all that I do and keep me from all trouble and pain!" and God granted him his request.

MOSES:

God used a continuously burning bush to get Moses' attention.[30] God chose Moses to lead the Israelites out of Egypt, away from their place of slavery, where they were not allowed to worship and serve their God. After their miraculous

---

[28] Genesis 17:1-8
[29] Genesis 32:22-32
[30] Exodus 3:2-3

exodus from Egypt, God brought them to Mount Sinai so He could reveal Himself to His people.[31]

Before their meeting could take place, the Israelites were required to cleanse themselves. On the third day of purification, God appeared. He revealed Himself to His people. It had been a long time since He had spoken of His love for them; so long since they had been in His presence.

Thunder reverberated throughout the land. Bolts of lightning flashed through the immense expanse of the sky. A dense cloud came down upon the mountain. God descended upon it, in the form of fire, and the smoke billowed into the sky, covering Mt. Sinai. The whole mountain shook.[32]

It was an incredible display of supremacy. Even the bravest of the brave could not stand erect. Deep terror paralyzed their hearts; intense fear shook their beings. The earth tremored. It brought so much fear upon the people that they begged God not to speak to them again. It was too much to have this almighty, holy God come into their presence. They took cover. The people knew they were sinful and did not want to stand before the almighty God. Intense dread seized their souls.

God never revealed Himself in that way again, but He did not go away. He did not leave mankind; His heart could not. Pure love perseveres. It is unconditional. It is both tender and powerful. God loves.

He selected Moses to speak on their behalf. God met with Moses and told him what to say to His people. When Moses went into the Tent of Meeting, a pillar of cloud descended. It hovered at the entrance when God spoke to Moses.[33] They communicated, face to face, just as friends do.[34]

---

[31] Exodus 19:9
[32] Exodus 19:16-20
[33] Exodus 33:9
[34] Exodus 33:11

After spending time with God, Moses' face glowed. But it was too bright and frightened the people. So, Moses wore a veil over his face.[35] God told Moses that He would go with him and would give Moses rest; everything would be fine.[36] Those were winning words, victorious words, - reassuring, comforting words.

But the Israelites chose not to trust God. As a result, the people wandered in the desert for forty years. God stayed with them, above them – visible by way of a cloud. During the day, this cloud covered the Tabernacle. Every morning when they woke, God was there in full sight. And at night, the cloud was illumined, it looked like a pillar of fire.[37] God did not hide; He was visible. God's presence was evident and He did not want His people to forget that He was with them – always. Though they wandered, He guided them by way of this cloud. When it lifted from the Tabernacle, the people broke camp and followed it. He was among them. They were His people and He was their God.

Exodus 29:45: I will live among the people and be their God and they will know that I am the Lord their God. I am the One who brought them out of the land of Egypt so that I could live among them. I am the Lord their God.

JUDGES:

Throughout the book of Judges, in the Old Testament, the Israelites continuously turned away from God. They chose to worship other gods in other religions, rather than believing in their Creator. Although they turned away from Him, God did not leave them in their rebellion. He was right there.

God handed the Israelites over to the neighbouring nations who oppressed them severely – until the Israelites

---

[35] Exodus 34:33-35
[36] Exodus 33:14
[37] Numbers 9:15-17

finally cried for help. "Oh God, deliver us!" God then ordained an Israelite to be judge and orchestrated victory and freedom from their oppressors. As long as the judge was alive, the people served God. But as soon as the judge died, the people returned to their evil and rebellious ways. Again, God allowed another nation to overpower the Israelites and used them as slaves, crushing them. After many years of hardship, they again cried out to God. And once again, God rescued them, by way of another judge. Over and over this cycle repeated itself, generation after generation.

Even though His rebellious people chose to follow other gods and ignore Him, God kept on wooing his people. He brought them back, but they continuously chose to reject Him. God was filled with love. He did whatever it took to be with His people. God did not give up; love pursued. God longed to be with His beloved people.

This pattern is true of us today. We tend to act like them. In our hard times, we cry out to God for help - "Please God." We make a promise, if only He would save us – and He does rescue us. It happens, we breathe – then we forget. We continue down our life's path, our way, until the next time. But God does not desert us, He waits – because He loves us. He longs to be accepted by us – always. Love never gives up.

Psalm 50:15 – Call upon Me in the day of trouble; I will deliver you
and you shall glorify Me.

A KING:

In time, God's people demanded to have a king who would rule them. They cried out for their own King, a leader like other nations had. They wanted a king they could talk to, reason with, one they could exalt – or kill. They wanted the power to elect their king. They wanted control. God knew they were rejecting Him as their leader, not wanting to follow Him anymore. He granted them their request. And He put His Spirit upon the rulers when they looked to Him for guidance. As history unfolded, some kings heeded God but many of them rebelled against Him. People worshiped other gods; sorrow filled God's heart.

Jeremiah 3:19 – I thought to myself," I would love to treat you as my own children! I wanted nothing more than to give you this beautiful land – the finest possession in the world. I look forward to you calling me 'Father' and I wanted you never to turn from me."

PROPHETS:
God found another way of speaking to His people. He appointed prophets, chosen men and women anointed to speak God's message. Sometimes God's words were heeded and sometimes they were rejected, but He kept speaking. He continuously told them of His everlasting love, never abandoning them. God displayed Himself in powerful ways.

Psalm 107:43 – Those who were wise will take all this to heart; they will see in our history the faithful love of the Lord.

- ## ELIJAH:
Elijah was a prophet of God who, after a great victory of God displaying His power, fled in fear of the King and Queen. Elijah obeyed God and now his life was in danger. He escaped into the mountains and a deep depression invaded his loneliness. He felt hopeless. God called Elijah to the mountain to reveal Himself.
  - A mighty windstorm tore the rocks from the mountain side, but God was not in the storm.
  - An earthquake shook the foundations of the earth.

- Then there was a ferocious fire. But God was not there.
- Finally, there was the sound of a gentle whisper, and Elijah knew: it was God.

Elijah's traumatized mind had heard the soft voice. His ringing ears and quaking soul detected the faint life-giving words of God. Elijah knew God was present. He covered his face before this holy God and their dialogue began.[38]

Psalm 37:7 – Be still in the presence of the Lord, and wait patiently for Him.

- **ISAIAH:**

Isaiah, another prophet, spoke of God's ever-present love for His people. God used the illustration of a mother and her child.[39] It is impossible for a nursing mother to forget her baby, for her breasts engorge with milk, causing pain that cannot be ignored. But, God said, even if it were possible for a nursing mother to fail to recall her child, He would never forget them, for He had tattooed their personal name on the palm of his hand. Tattooing was permanent. Its mark was embedded into the layers of skin. God's love for, and to, His people was everlasting. His love was from the core of His heart. His image was imprinted in them, in us. Our name is tattooed on the palm of His hand. Forever. For always.

Isaiah reassured God's people not to be afraid, for God called them by name. They were His. When they went through deep waters, God was with them. When they went through rivers of difficulty, they would not drown. When they walked through the fire of oppression, they would not

---

[38] 1 Kings 19:11-13
[39] Isaiah 49:15-16

burn, for He was their God.[40] How tender His love was for His people. Over and over God proclaimed that He was with them, loved them. His people rebelled, worshiped other gods, rejected Him. And yet, He still hovered over them, longing for His people's love.

Isaiah 46:3-4 – I have cared for you since you were born. Yes, I carried you before you were born. I will be your God throughout your lifetime - until your hair is white with age. I made you, and I will care for you. I will carry you along and save you.

- **HOSEA:**
Hosea was a prophet through whom God demonstrated His love for His people. In the book of Hosea, God directs Hosea to marry a prostitute. He obeyed. As time proceeded, his wife left him for other men. She sought the arms of other lovers, not his. Hosea was rejected. Betrayed. God told Hosea to buy her back. Hosea scoured the streets until he located her. He purchased his wife, rescuing her from the embraces of men who used her. He bought her back; his wife became his again. She was his legally, twice over. God displayed His unfailing love for His people through the illustration of Hosea's life.

Hosea 2:20 – I will be faithful to you and make you mine, and you will finally know Me as the Lord.

A JEALOUS LOVER
God described Himself as compassionate, full of loving kindness, patient and slow to anger.[41] He also declared that His name is Jealous.[42] He viewed His people as His prized

---

[40] Isaiah 43:1-2
[41] Exodus 34:6-7
[42] Exodus 34:14

possession,[43] and does not want them to form allegiance with any other being or thing. God pleaded with His people to repent of their sin and return to Him. He longed to be their Lover. He fought fiercely for them, yet gave them choice, the freedom to reject Him.

Isaiah 65:1 –The Lord God said, "I was ready to respond, but no one asked for help. I was ready to be found, but no one was looking for me. I said, 'Here I am, here I am!' to a nation that did not call on My name.

God continuously pursued mankind – like an obsessed lover. God had His arms wide open to them, yet the people followed their own rebellious and crooked ways. How His heart cried out for them and yet they rejected Him. He was constantly waiting. He waited for His people in the Old Testament and He waits for us now. For you. For me. He is the same yesterday, today and all our tomorrows.[44]

Over and over throughout history, God revealed His heart of absolute delight for His people, longing for the people created in His image. His plan is for each of us to have an intimate relationship with Him. Come, let Him touch your tender soul. The choice is yours. He is right beside you, waiting to hold your heart and fill it with His deep, warm, secure love. It is the ultimate story of love.

PRAYER:
Dear God. I didn't realize that You have always loved me, even when I walked away from you. Thank you for not giving up on me. I choose to turn from my own ways and follow You. I open my heart to you; I receive your love for me. Fill my heart to overflowing with your Presence. Thank you for loving me so very much. Thank you for being my God.

---

[43] Exodus 19:5
[44] Hebrews 13:8

44

I have loved you with an everlasting love.

With unfailing love,

I have drawn you to myself.

- Jeremiah 31:3

REFLECTIONS: Chapter 3 – The Story of Love

1. How would you describe 'love'?
   What is conditional and unconditional love?
2. How did God display His love when Adam disobeyed?
3. How did God show His love to: Enoch? Noah? Abraham? Jacob? Moses? To the Israelites? During the time of the Judges? In giving them a king? Elijah? Isaiah? Hosea?
4. How do you know that God loves you?
5. God longs to pour His love into your heart.
   Open your heart and let Him pour His love into it.
   Ask Him daily to fill your heart with His amazing love.

Notes & Journaling:

_____

_____

_____

_____

_____

_____

_____

_____

_____

_____

_____

Chapter 4

The Plan

He was quite the man, with a plan.
Played with death.
Possible fatality.
Possible explosion.
A possible end - six feet under.
In pieces.

Alfred Nobel was a persistent man. Some considered him
unstable. Careless. Crazy. Playing with his life. Onlookers
called it Russian roulette, inviting an unpredictable death. But
day after day, month after month, Nobel kept experimenting
with nitroglycerin. This colourless liquid appeared to be
harmless but it was highly explosive. Its molecules were
extremely unstable. In its raw form, even so much as the
slightest jolt or impact would cause it to spontaneously
detonate. Friction rearranged the molecules, causing it to
explode. It was lethal if not moved properly.[45] Mishandling it
invited certain death.

Nobel was banned to a barge when performing his
experiments. It was too dangerous to work with nitroglycerin
among people. His brother and several other men died while
handling it. But Alfred Nobel did not die. He knew nitroglycerin
was powerful and could be useful – when handled with care.
He knew something his brother did not know. Every detail was
critical and had to be carried out with precision or the result
would be fatal. Any missed detail would result in death.

---

[45] Imperial College London, An Explosive Combination of Atoms, n.d.,
http://www.ch.ic.ac.uk/rzepa/mim/environmental/html/nitroglyc_text.htm

Nobel discovered how to handle nitroglycerin without it exploding. His experimentation revealed that, when nitroglycerin was mixed with another element, an emulsifier, it became stable and could be stored safely without fear of exploding. This process was closely monitored so that a detonation was extremely unlikely.[46] His plan worked. In 1867, Alfred Nobel patented his product as dynamite.[47]

The holiness of God is infinitely purer and more powerful than nitroglycerin. In the Old Testament, mishandling the holiness of God resulted in death. Life was snuffed out – like an extinguished candle.

In II Samuel 6, King David planned for the priests to bring the Ark of Covenant back to its homeland. It was not an ordinary container; the presence of our holy God was within. It had to be handled with care, very specifically – just like nitroglycerin. All conditions had to be met perfectly.

The anticipated day arrived and it was a great day of celebration. Such joy. Extreme elation. Excitement vibrated throughout the people's hearts. King David's deep desire was coming true: the presence of God was returning home, to the City of David. After many years of absence, it was coming back where it was supposed to be.

With great anticipation, they loaded the Ark of Covenant onto a cart, pulled by oxen. And they were off, over the terrain, heading to where it belonged. Home. But the cart hit a bump and the Ark nearly fell off. A man reached out his hand to steady it. Death ambushed the scene, striking the man who touched the Ark. It was a fatal touch. Death robbed him of his life.

In their haste to get the Ark of Covenant back to the City of David, important information had been forgotten. God had specified how to transport the Ark of the Covenant. It was not

---

[46] Carey Sublette, How is liquid nitroglycerin stored? 2017, quora.com
[47] Ibid.

to be placed on a cart pulled by oxen, but instead carried with inserted poles by the Levites.[48] Nobody was allowed to touch it. Nobody. The Ark was to be respected, revered as holy, untouchable. But God's instructions were ignored, making it fatal for this one man. Death claimed him; it cost him his life.

Our God is holy and He cannot be taken lightly. God's holiness has no hint of impurity, it holds no blemish. None – not even a trace or a hint of darkness. He is our holy God and His holiness is powerful, far surpassing any quantity of nitroglycerin.

Isaiah cried out, "Woe is me for I am a man of unclean lips!"[49] Sin overwhelmed him, it suffocated his breath of life. Guilt invaded peace. Overpowered it. Defeated it. Made him unclean.

- God, the great I AM – sacred and pure.
- Mankind is fickle – rebellious and defiant.

Holiness and sin cannot co-exist, without intervention.

Together they are as oil and water. Polarization makes them antagonistic, their molecular makeup inhibiting connection. Oil and water cannot co-exist – unless shaken, blending the two. But shaking is a temporary mix, for the heaviness of water again separates these two elements over time.

Just so, in the Old Testament, God had a plan in which mankind could be purified of sin, but it was temporary. It was possible to come before our holy God – without dying. There was a way that sin could be dealt with – for a while. It was through the repetitive offering of sacrifices.

Hebrews 10:11 – Under the old covenant, the priest stands ~~and ministers~~ before the alter day after day, offering the same sacrifices again and again, which can never take away sins.

---

[48] Numbers 4:15
[49] Isaiah 6:5

There were many types of sacrifices for intentional and unintentional sin. The burnt offering was made for the forgiveness and cleansing of sin. The debt of guilt required life blood as payment for the offence. When a sacrifice was made, it took on the weight of a person's guilt so they became acceptable to God – but only for a while. Every year the high priest would offer another sacrifice, the shedding of blood, to cover the nation's sin.

Hebrews 9:22 – According to the law of Moses, . . . without the shedding of blood, there is no forgiveness.

A sacrifice opened the possibility of being acceptable to the holy God. The people would be safe. They needed their God, desperately needed Him. He was their source of life. God gave them detailed instructions. Under the Law of Moses, there were very specific requirements that had to be performed and completed in order for His people to live, avoiding death.

Sacrifices took time and planning. They were made in a specific place, at a specific time, by a specific person. There were no exceptions. Both the offering, as well as the one who offered, had to go through steps of purification. Purity was crucial. The sacrificial animal had to be without defect, without blemish, no trace of imperfection.

The descendants of Aaron were set apart as priests, to minister to God. They became the mediators between God and His people,[50] performing the sacrifices and keeping all the requirements of God. They had specific clothing to wear, and needed to be very careful when offering sacrifices – first dealing with their own sin, then offering sacrifices on behalf of the people. If God's explicit instructions were not followed, His holiness would consume them. Obedience was important.

---

[50] Exodus 29:1-9

Aaron's two sons, Nadab and Abihu, were priests who ignored God's instructions in regards to offering a sacrifice. As a result, fire blazed from God's presence and they died.[51] They had disregarded the seriousness of God's holiness. Obedience determined life, or death.

Fulfilling the requirements made it possible for God to live among them,[52] without the penalty of death. God longed to inhabit a place among them, so, when the tabernacle was built, He gave meticulous instructions on how to build it and furnish it.[53] At the inner core of the tabernacle, and later the Temple, was the Holy of Holies. This was where the presence of God dwelt. A heavy curtain separated this holy place from the rest of the building. No one dared enter that place except the high priest, for the annual sacrifice. This sacrifice was extremely important, for it cleansed the people from their sin – for another year. Sacrifices covered their sins for the time being. They had no permanent solution to erase their guilt.

Let us think again of the container of oil and water. No matter how many times it was shaken, it always separated in time. However, it was discovered that if, a certain substance, an emulsifier, was added, the two elements were capable of bonding.[54] With an emulsifier, oil and water could co-exist, connect, forever. No shaking necessary.

Our emulsifier's name is Jesus Christ, being both God and man. This 'God-Man' is the perfect emulsifier. Jesus is God, pure and holy. When He came to Earth, He put aside all His rights, as God, to come in the form of a man. God's holy presence, through Jesus, could now dwell with sinful people.

While on the cross, Jesus cried out, "It is finished!" The final payment had been made; the debt was completely

---

[51] Leviticus 10:1-2
[52] Exodus 25:8
[53] Exodus 25:8
[54] Sarah Zielinski, Oil and Water do Mix, 2010, smithsonianmag.com

.. No payments were left to be made. Sacrifices are no ⸗r necessary. It is done, completely fulfilled. The death of ⸗sus satisfied the debt of sin. It covered all our guilt. That was God's plan. We can now be with Him – forever. Because of Jesus, we can dwell in God's presence and live. What an incredible plan - God's gift of mercy. Amazing love.

Ephesians 1:4-5 - Even before God made the world; He loved us and chose us in Christ to be holy and without fault in His eyes. He had a plan to adopt us into His own family by bringing us to Himself through Jesus Christ. This is what He wanted to do and it gave Him great pleasure.

God knew that mankind would sin because of free choice, but He had a plan. The plan was to send His only Son, Jesus Christ, to the earth, to be the final sacrifice for the sins of mankind. His Son, Jesus, was the ultimate, pure sacrifice who would give up His blood in payment for our sins.

John 3:16 – For God loved the world so much that He gave His one and only Son, so that everyone who believes in Him will not perish but have eternal life.

When we accept this payment, we are cleansed and made holy before God, acceptable to Him. God's plan was designed and accomplished because of His passionate love for us. Love is who He is. His love compelled Him to send His Son, Jesus, to die for us.

I John 4:12 – . . . His love is brought to full expression in us.

This was God's passion: giving His Son to die, so that you and I are able to have a relationship with Him. This relationship is not ordinary but one of adoption. We belong together. This was His plan, and it gave Him great pleasure.[55]

What a plan. Brilliant. Indisputable. Yet His plan came with tremendous cost – His Son endured a cruel and undeserved death on a cross. God the Father, so loved us, that He sacrificed His Son for us.

I John 4:9-10 - God showed how much He loved us by sending His one and only Son into the world so that we might have eternal life through Him. This is real love – not that we loved God, but that He loved us and sent His Son as a sacrifice to take away our sins.

Jesus was more than an honourable Teacher who walked the earth. He was the Son of God. He died, resurrected, then became alive again. For the next forty days, He walked with people again, ate the fish that was given to Him. He spoke. He touched people once again. He had risen in victory, triumphant over the clutches of sin and the sting of death. God knew that the intense pain of sending His beloved Son to die, an excruciating death, would result in glorious resurrection and unite mankind with Himself – forever. Jesus is our Emulsifier.

Romans 5:8, 11 – But God showed His great love for us by sending Christ to die for us while we were still sinners. . . So now we can rejoice in our wonderful new relationship with God because our Lord Jesus Christ has made us friends of God.

This was God's magnificent plan. How glorious. Amazing. God knew before our existence that we would choose to sin. He had a plan; His plan came with a price. The cost of His Son's death was worth the glorious consequence of having intimacy with mankind. God's plan trumped the darkness – victoriously. Once again, God was able to walk with His people, with us.

---

[55] Ephesians 1:5

PRAYER:

Oh Lord! You knew that I would sin and you made a way for me to come to You, to be acceptable to You. What an amazing plan You made for me! Thank you, dear Lord. Thank you for loving me. I want to walk with you. I'm coming!

We can boldly enter heaven's Most Holy place
because of the blood of Jesus. By His death,
Jesus opened a new and life-giving way
through the curtain into the Most Holy place.
And since we have a great High Priest
who rules over God's house,
let us go right into the presence of God
with sincere hearts fully trusting Him.
For our guilty consciences have been sprinkled
with Christ's blood
to make us clean and our bodies have been
washed with pure water.
- Hebrews 10:19-22

Reflections: Chapter 4 – The Plan

1. How does nitroglycerin demonstrate the holiness of God?
2. How could the Old Testament people become acceptable to God?
3. Why did God have such strict regulations in order to be accepted by Him?
4. What is an emulsifier?
   How does it work?
5. How is Jesus our 'emulsifier'?
6. How does it feel to have a 'Papa' Father?

Notes & Journaling:

_____

_____

_____

_____

_____

_____

_____

_____

_____

_____

_____

_____

_____

_____

_____

_____

_____

_____

_____

_____

_____

PART 3

Enabling Experience

Jesus is a gentleman;
He waits to be welcomed
into our lives.

We receive the gift
of forgiveness and in turn,
offer forgiveness
to our offenders.

When we give Jesus our guilt, shame, and
anger,
we are able to experience
His Presence.

Chapter 5

Human Will and the Door

In August 2008, twenty-seven-year old Amanda Lindhout's terror of 15 months began. She was held hostage in Somalia.[56]

Imagine:
- being captured, trapped.
- being controlled against your will, overpowered.
- being oppressed, beaten, sexually abused, starved.
- being without a voice, unheard.
- being helpless, with no choice.
- being vulnerable, unprotected and alone.

Day after day. Night after night. It continued for 459 days and nights, before the ransom was paid. She was finally released. Free of the merciless acts and words of her captors – men who did whatever they wanted with her. She had been forced to obey with no mercy.

Jesus is not like that. He does not force us to obey Him. He could – but He does not. He is a gentleman. He respects us, gives us the power to choose. We can do anything we want; we have choice.

Ms. Lindhout, too, had choice. At one point she contemplated using a razor to end her life.[57] Choosing to live was too much; she longed to give up. But a little bird flew into her cell and it filled her soul with hope. She chose to live – and she did.

---

[56] Joseph Brean, Amanda Lindhout's Terrifying 15 Months as a Hostage in Somalia, National Post, June 12, 2015, nationalpost.com
[57] Ibid.

When we choose, consequences follow. We have freedom to choose our attitude, in the midst of what is happening to us, no matter how dire the situation. We have the power to chose how we will respond. We are responsible for our thoughts, our words and actions, regardless of the circumstance. Choice is powerful. Choice determines our life path.

Many years ago, I stood in front of a famous painting called *Light of the World* [58] in St. Paul's Cathedral, London, UK. This well-known masterpiece, painted by William Holman Hunt, in 1851, symbolizes the love brought by Jesus to everyone, everywhere. Jesus is standing at an overgrown and unopened door. His right hand is preparing to knock on the door while His left hand is holding a lantern. There is no handle on the outside of this door. The inscription below the painting is Revelation 3:20, which says: 'Behold, I stand at the door and knock. If any man hears my voice and opens the door, I will come in to him and sup with him and he with me.'

Even though God is the Architect of the door, He positioned Himself externally. Man is given the ability to rationalize and choose. Jesus has made it possible for us to be with Him but He does not force anyone against their wishes – no obligation, no coercion, no manipulation. He purposely designed the door without an outside handle.

Fifty years after painting this picture, artist Hunt felt that he should explain why that door had no outside handle. Hunt stated that the door represented 'the obstinately shut mind',[59] symbolizing the human mind, a mind that is firmly and stubbornly padlocked. This unyielding attitude cannot be controlled or overcome easily, for it displays inflexible persistence.

---

[58] St. Paul's Cathedral, The Light of the World, n.d., stpauls.co.uk
[59] Ibid.

Jesus keeps knocking on the door of our heart because He loves us – dearly. When Jesus came to Earth, He gave up all rights as God. He emptied Himself of His divine state and its privileges, by humbling Himself to the position of a slave.[60] He was born as a human being, subject to the conditions that sin had caused within mankind. The great I AM had subjected Himself to the chaos of mankind's sinful condition. He chose to live among His created beings, amid their free choice, in the midst of sin. His body was subject to all the elements that brought pain and discomfort.

He understands us, wants to come alongside of us. That is why He keeps knocking. Tirelessly, He tries to get our attention. Free choice is freedom to choose. His love consumes His heart. He longs to enter to share a meal with us, to have fellowship with us. But we have control of the door, so He waits.

When God described Himself in Exodus, He stated that He was slow to anger.[61] God has a good reason to be angry when we rebel against Him. It does not mean that He will not get angry, for there are recorded incidents where God was furious:

- He was angry with Aaron for allowing the Israelites to make a golden calf idol for worship and He wanted to destroy them.[62]
- King David experienced the anger of God, then wrote a psalm of celebration stating that God's anger lasts only a moment, but His favour lasts a lifetime.[63]

God is slow to get angry. The patience of God gives people the opportunity to be saved from their sin. He provides people the opportunity to turn to Him.

---

[60] Philippians 2:7
[61] Exodus 34:6
[62] Deuteronomy 9:20
[63] Psalm 30:5

II Peter 3:9 – The Lord isn't really being slow about His promise, as some people think. No, He is being patient for your sake. He does not want anyone to be destroyed but wants everyone to repent.

Jesus is knocking on every heart's door. He died for our sin. Jesus did not die more for the murderer than the one whose life displays holiness. We are all guilty. Any tiny mark of sin makes each of us impure. It does not matter how big the mark. Each of us are favored with the undeserved unconditional presence of Jesus. First God created us, then He ransomed us, by buying us back with the blood of His Son, Jesus. We are His prized possessions. He sacrificed His everything and endured immense suffering for every person.

In the Old Testament, God had His 'chosen' people, called the Israelites. But His mercy and love were not limited to them.

STORY OF JONAH:

God told Jonah to go to the pagan capital city of the Assyrian Empire, called Nineveh, to plead with them to repent. This nation was cruel and ruthless. Jonah wanted them destroyed, not saved. He refused to obey God and preach repentance. God had him swallowed by a massive fish, and after three days in its putrid dark innards, Jonah finally agreed to go and preach to the wicked city of Nineveh. When he called the city to repent, the people fasted and were remorseful of their malicious behaviour. God heard them and abandoned His plan to destroy them. He had knocked on their hearts' door. They heard Him and let Him in.

Repentance is offered to everyone. Every person is invited to celebrate life with Him. Forgiveness of sin is a gift to one and all. There is no exception. We have all sinned and come short of meeting God's requirements of holiness.[64] Jesus is persistent. He treasures every heart. He keeps knocking.

The Bible states that people turn to human reasoning and false arguments; they lean heavily on their own understanding. These obstacles keep them from knowing God.[65] Their thoughts are rebellious against the knowledge of God, opposing the truth. Their senses are deadened and they step into the devil's trap. They have become captive to themselves[66] because they have barricaded the door from the inside. They hold themselves hostage.

Out of curiosity, I was eager to learn if it was illegal to barricade yourself inside your home. I discovered that it is perfectly legal, as long as the police are not requiring you to come out. You can stay as long as you want within the barricade.[67] It is your home, your place. You can choose how long you want to stay confined in the space of your heart with the door locked shut. You hold the key. You determine entrance. You give permission to who enters and when they enter. Jesus will not bash against the door of our heart. He will not ram against the door as soldiers did in days of old, forcing open the city gates. Jesus is a gentleman, and gives us freedom of choice, whether to open the door or not.

There are several barricades that block the door of our heart:
1. ANGER:
When anger becomes the bodyguard within the soul, it blocks the door. Anger obstructs ears from hearing. Anger is a wall built to protect against further pain and injustice. The poison of anger can keep Jesus from entering.

- Milo recalled his painful memory. When asked if he could sense Jesus, he responded with an adamant, "No". I asked

---

[64] Romans 3:23
[65] 2 Corinthians 10:3-5
[66] 2 Timothy 2:25-26
[67] Answers.yaho.com

him if he sensed any anger to which he stated, "Oh, yes!" We explored the anger and he decided that he did not want the anger anymore. He gave it to Jesus, along with the person whom he was angry with. When he went back to the memory, he saw Jesus. He was present. The young man received healing and freedom when he finally chose to get rid of the blockade of anger. Jesus entered his heart.

- Ian lost his business, family, home and possessions, because of his drinking. His self worth was non-existent. He felt he was a loser and stupid. He sensed Jesus but did not want to hear Him. Ian knew that Jesus wanted to help, but Ian turned his back on Jesus. He was angry at God for not stopping him from drinking, angry at himself for continuing to drink. Ian became tired of living in the hurricane of anger within his soul. During his Inner Healing Session, Ian chose to face Jesus and welcomed Him into his life. Ian let go of the anger towards God and forgave himself. Peace flooded into his soul.

Psalm 4:4 – Don't sin by letting anger control you. Think about it overnight and remain silent.

2. STUBBORNNESS AND PRIDE:

Stubbornness keeps the door bolted shut, while pride sits on the throne. Jesus is not allowed entrance. As long as no one is permitted in, the throne is theirs. God stated that stubbornness is as worshipping idols.[68] That sounds similar to the history of the Israelites during the period of the judges. They refused to honour God.

Pride is a powerful barricade. When Jesus was on Earth, He spoke in parables, hiding the truth from those who considered themselves wise.[69] Over and over God spoke,

---

[68] 1 Samuel 15:23

saying we must have the humbleness of a child. He leads the humble.[69] God urges us to humble ourselves before Him.[71] Pride barricades the entrance of Jesus.

- Jeremy realized as a young boy that when he threw a tantrum, he would get his way. From then on, his family gave him whatever his heart desired. He became a golden boy. Then he entered the real world. When his first girlfriend relationship ended, he succumbed to deep depression. It happened again and again, girlfriend two, three and four. The seeming bottomless pit of depression led to drinking and a life out of control. In his adult life, he realized how damaging his stubbornness and pride were.

- Scott stubbornly held a lot of anger within himself. When he was young, his mother had accused him of doing something that he was not guilty of. He loathed his mom. He believed that when she stands before God someday, she would realize that her son had been speaking the truth. He stubbornly refused to forgive her, although it made him miserable. He was stuck in the futility of holding his mom accountable for not believing him as a little boy. His stubbornness and pride kept Jesus from entering his heart and lifting his burden of pain.

Proverbs 16:18 – Pride goes before destruction and haughtiness before a fall.

3. GUILT AND SHAME:
When there is guilt and shame hanging onto your being, it may be difficult to welcome Jesus. You feel unworthy and ashamed. But Jesus knows everything about you and He adores you. He understands. He is gentle and compassionate.

---

[69] Matthew 11:25
[70] Psalm 25:9
[71] James 4:6,10

He has already paid for your guilt; receive His forgiveness. Give Him your coat of shame. Open the door and look into His eyes. He passionately loves you.

- Ernie remembered being a little boy, in the school bathroom, utterly humiliated by the teacher. Shame filled his heart. He felt that he was not good enough and would never be liked. In the bathroom, darkness surrounded Ernie, shame suffocated him. By Grade Six, rage took over his being and he was known as a violent boy. Life was extremely difficult.

When I asked him where Jesus was in the memory, Ernie replied that He was outside the school house where it was bright. He invited Jesus into the room. Jesus told him that it was not his fault, that the shame was never his to carry. Jesus went on to say that shame is like holding on to a rotten piece of meat. Ernie broke down in tears as he gave Jesus his shame. He had held onto it for much too long. When Ernie went back to the memory, it was no longer paralyzing. He remembered it all, but now it was a peaceful memory.

Isaiah 54:4 – Fear not; you will no longer live in shame. Don't be afraid; there is no more disgrace for you. You will no longer remember the shame of your youth . . ..

4. FEAR:

Being afraid holds you back from changing anything. When your heart is full of terror, any opened door may allow more chaos to enter, more vulnerability to wound your heart. Jesus understands. Let Him in so that He can bring healing into your soul. His words, 'Fear not, for I am with you', will bring deep comfort into your soul. He knows all about you and loves you deeply. He can take away your fear. Let Him come into your life. He adores you. He is with you. Trust Him.

Psalm 27:1 – The Lord is my light and my salvation – so why should I be afraid? The Lord is my fortress, protecting me from danger, so why should I tremble?

Some people are unaware of the barricades they have built to protect themselves. It shields them from being hurt – again. The pain of isolation outweighs the possibility of more hurt. But the soul slowly dies. And all the while Jesus is knocking at the door. Give Him a chance. Let Him in. Instead of feeling coldness and condemnation, accept His warmth. The radiance of His life-giving light overtakes the suffocating darkness.

After an Inner Healing Session of releasing anger, guilt, and shame, I have often witnessed a person opening their eyes and exclaiming that the room was so much brighter. Jesus had been invited into their life; the darkness dissipated. Life radiated with the love of Jesus' presence.

MY HEART'S DOOR:

When I open the door of my heart to Jesus, His peace flows in, like a mighty river. It is powerful. His peace engulfs any disturbance of what is going on around me. Jesus' presence breaths serenity into the depth of my soul.

It happened the night before my daughter died, as I was sitting at her feet. Her hospital room was located at the end of the corridor, so I was able to see some activity down the hall. I observed people pushing a stretcher out of a room – on it was a bagged body. I knew that someone had died. My eyes took in the scene as an observer, but the sting of death was not able to penetrate my soul. Jesus was my shield. There was calmness, deep within my heart. Nothing could penetrate His peace; nothing could taint it. No power of darkness could overtake the presence of His light. I knew that He was with me. His presence radiated peace, for He held me secure. I knew that I would be okay.

That night, Jesus was the guard at the door of my heart. He was standing on the inside, not the outside. I had given Him the key to my heart's door. I chose for Him to be on the throne within my being. I trusted Him. I adored Him.

If you are in the midst of one of life's storms, invite Jesus into your heart. He absolutely adores you. He understands your fears and waits calmly for your invitation. His words will drive the darkness away; His peace will flood into your being. Sweet and tender peace.

Open your heart's door in response to His knocking. He is waiting for you to welcome Him into your heart. You will not be disappointed. His presence satisfies the desires of your heart. Your soul will find healing and a freedom to live. Peace will flow within your being.

PRAYER:

Oh Lord, I am so sorry for not opening the door of my heart sooner. I didn't realize what I was doing by not letting you come in the door. I really need you. I'm lonely and it's so dark inside my soul. I open my heart's door and welcome You. I need your peace. Come in, dear Lord Jesus. Thank you for loving me so very much, and that You died for my guilt. Fill me with your peace. Come talk with me. Fill my heart with your warm Presence. Come in, dear Jesus. Fill me with your amazing love. I ask this in the name of Jesus, Amen.

My heart has heard you say,

"Come and talk with Me."

And my heart responds,

"Lord, I am coming."

- Psalm 27:8

REFLECTIONS: Chapter 5 – The Human Will and the Door

1. What is the significance of having no handle on the outside of the door?
2. What does it feel like to have Jesus knocking at your door?
3. What keeps people from opening their heart's door?
4. How does anger keep Jesus out?
   What about stubbornness and pride?
   Guilt and shame?
   Fear?
5. What does it feel like to have Jesus in your heart?
   Take time to sit with Him. Talk with Him.
   Receive His love.

Notes & Journaling:

_____

_____

_____

_____

_____

_____

_____

_____

_____

_____

_____

_____

_____

_____

Chapter 6

Forgiven!

It is not uncommon for a family to have two siblings that are completely different. It might appear that they are not related – but they are. Their DNA came from the same gene pool.

So begins the story of a father who had two sons. They were completely and profoundly different. The eldest son was tall, thin, and dark with brown eyes; the other son had freckles, green eyes, and the body of a wrestler. One was studious while the other had no interest in learning. The older son was responsible while the younger son was reckless.

Their father scratched his head, wondering how he could influence the younger son to build a better life. He tried talking to his son, telling him of his incredible potential but his son had his own plans. He wanted to see the world, and experience it at its fullest. He did not want to work with his father, in construction.

Once the decision was made, nobody could change this son's mind. He was leaving, leaving his dad and brother, leaving his boring life. Taking the money his father had given him to start his own construction company, he said a brief goodbye, and left.

The son ignored the sadness in his father's eyes, eyes that expressed love to him. He only saw eyes that limited him. He was going out on his own to live. Really live.

The son jumped into his jacked-up pickup truck, shifted gears, released the clutch and was gone. He was going into the city where the lights never shut off. His father watched the vehicle as it sped down the driveway and out onto the road.

His eyes filled with tears. He feared for his son's life. Letting go was so hard and it tore at his heart, crushing his soul. Compassion welled up within his being for he loved his son, and now his son was gone. The father said a prayer that rose up into heaven, "I know you are with him, O Lord. Please protect him. I want to see him again. Please Lord."

Very soon, the 'good life' devoured the son – chewed him up, then vomited him out. His new, so-called friends had used him and betrayed him. He was cut to the core of his being – rejected. His money was gone. The streets became his refuge; the garbage bins were his pantry.

One day, he was sitting on the sidewalk, hand outstretched for change. A man stopped and looked at him, without condemnation, just compassion. Not pity, but love. Eyes so like those of his father.

The young man's face dropped in shame. Guilt locked an iron fist around his throat. Its massive hands choked the breath from him. Guilt greedily sucked life from his being, deflated his purpose, extinguished all hope.

He saw the man's boot full of mud. That was his life. Mud and dirt. He covered his watering eyes with his hands and tears began to flow. His chest heaved. He felt doomed. Hopelessness consumed his soul. He was alone. Desperately alone. He saw himself alone – forever.

A gentle hand touched his shoulder. "I'm here", said the man. "How can I help you? Do you have a family?"

"Yes, I do have a family."

"Would you like to go home?" the man asked.

"Oh yes!" replied the young man. "But I don't know if my dad will ever speak to me again. I've been really inconsiderate. I spent all the money he gave me. He trusted me with the money, to start my own company. I've failed him, having recklessly spent it all. I really miss him."

"Would you go home if you had a way?"

"Oh yes! But it's far away. I have no money." Tears trickled from his sorrowful green eyes. His lips were dry, parched.

"I will buy you a bus ticket. But you must promise me that you will start to live your life with purpose. Go home to your dad and do whatever he says."

"Really? You would do that for me?" The man nodded and the young man continued. "I will! I will! I promise! Thank you. Thank you so much."

The young man looked upon the tender face in front of him. He looked into his eyes. Eyes that spoke of love and hope; eyes that were soft and not condemning.

"I will make my dad proud. If only he talks to me again. I will do anything that he wants. I want to see him." This young man cried out, "Please God, please help my dad to forgive me. I need to be okay again. Please God. I'm so sorry. Please forgive me."

The stranger purchased a bus ticket and placed it into the young man's hand. His heart was filled with gratefulness when he lifted his eyes to the heavens and prayed, "One more chance. I just need this one more chance. Please God."

He stepped onto the bus and waved to the stranger. A smile adorned his face as the bus weaved its way through the streets, maneuvering out into the country, navigating its way to his hometown.

The young man said, once again, "One more chance. God, I am only asking for one more chance."

That particular day, his father was working up on a rooftop, laying down shingles and thinking of his beloved son, longing for him to come home. It was a very hot day. Beads of sweat oozed from his forehead. They trickled down into his bushy eyebrows. He stood up to give his back a rest and scanned the area.

He saw the figure of a man walking down the sidewalk. He looked familiar yet this man's walk was different – slower, methodical. The father tried to make out the man's face but it was covered by the hood of his jacket. Then the man on the sidewalk paused and wiped his nose – with the back of his hand – just like his son used to. The father's heart began pounding. His eyes strained to see who it was. Sweat stung his eyes.

The father stared. His eyes were riveted on the young man walking down the street. 'It must be him. It surely looks like him,' he thought. The father moved to the edge of the roof, and with trembling feet descended the ladder.

The young man was much closer when his father's voice trembled, in hope, "Son? Son, is that you?" His eyes lingered on the face. The face that held green eyes. It was his son! "My sonnn!!" The father bolted and grabbed the young man, his huge arms held him tightly. Oh, how he loved his son. He came back. Forgiveness oozed from the father's heart, flowing into the young man's heart.

Forgiveness deals with guilt. Forgiveness is necessary. We are like this son, in need of forgiveness. All of us have gone our own way. We have all sinned and the penalty of sin is death.

We were doomed, that was, until someone took over the debt of sin. Our guilt was transferred to a new owner, Jesus. He fully paid our debt with His blood and that is why He cried out, "It is finished!" The last payment had been made. Jesus does not have to die again and again every time we sin. The death of Jesus fully satisfied our penalty of death. Now there is no reason to offer any more sacrifices.

Hebrews 10:2,10,18 – If they (sacrifices) could have provided perfect cleansing, the sacrifices would have stopped, for the worshipers would have been purified once for all time; and their feelings of guilt would have disappeared. . . For God's will was for us to be made holy by the sacrifice of the body of Jesus Christ, once for all time. . .

When sins have been forgiven, there is no need to offer any more sacrifices.

Jesus, the Son of God, made forgiveness possible. Our guilt is covered. We become acceptable to God, purified by the blood of Jesus. Forgiveness is a gift of God's great love to you, and me.

Colossians 1:21-22 – This includes you who were once far away from God. You were His enemies, separated from Him by your evil thoughts and actions. Yet now He has reconciled you to Himself through the death of Christ in His physical body. As a result, He has brought you into His own presence, and you are holy and blameless as you stand before Him without a single fault.

No wonder God the Father was excited with His ultimate plan for intimate communion with mankind. His heart was bursting with eagerness when He sent His Son, Jesus, to this world.
- No wonder He sent a host of angels proclaiming the birth of the Messiah baby.[72]
- No wonder God spoke in an audible voice when His Son Jesus was baptized, saying, "You are my dearly loved Son, and you bring me great joy."[73]

His plan was in motion and the ultimate desire of His heart was unfolding. It was happening; it was time. The pinnacle of His plan was taking place.

Instead of God being obscure, He became flesh so He could identify with us, and us with Him. God allowed mankind to look upon Him, His face was visible. He was not a spirit that could not be seen. God felt hunger, sorrow, and weariness through Jesus, and He was tempted just as we are.[74]

---

[72] Luke 2:1-14
[73] Mark 1:11
[74] Hebrews 4:15

God walked with those He had created. Jesus touched people, spoke to them, and ate with them. He was known as the One who welcomed the outcast into His presence. He went into the homes of those who were considered the scum of society. He ate with cheaters, liars, and losers. He honoured women, although they were considered undesirable, not worthy. He spoke with street people, workers, the rich rulers, and prostitutes. Children were drawn to Him. They sensed His gentleness and He delighted in them.

While on Earth, Jesus experienced the emotions that are within us, His humanness felt pain and disappointment. He uttered grief when His friend Lazarus died.[75] He wept in the presence of others, allowing them to see his tears. He had no shame in His compassion.

There had been no other teacher like Jesus. His words held power. His teachings touched thousands of people. He dared to speak out; His words were different than anything the people had ever heard. Jesus demonstrated His words; He lived His words.

Jesus was not an ordinary man, He demonstrated authority:
- The waves and wind obeyed Him. Instantly.
- He commanded sickness to leave. It dissipated.
- Demons were cast out. They fled.
- Jesus exposed the corruptness of the spiritual leaders. They hated Him.

The religious leaders made laws, putting heavy burdens on the people in order to fulfill manmade rules of acceptability to God. Jesus spoke to the masses, asking them to come to God – to receive freedom.

One day, the religious leaders brought a woman before Jesus. She was not an ordinary woman. She was considered a prostitute, and was looked down upon as guilty, dirty, and

---

[75] John 11:35

worthless. They wanted to trap Jesus, stump Him, accuse Him of not keeping the Law if she was not stoned.

He looked at the leaders with piercing eyes, then tenderly looked at the woman. His eyes were soft, life-giving, and compassionate. Then He spoke, "The one who is without sin, can throw the first stone."

The religious leaders studied each other, then looked at the gathering crowd. A pile of stones was ready to be thrown. Different shapes and sizes. Some heavy, some lighter. The rocks called out to them, "Pick me up! Throw me! You need to get rid of this sin, this sinful woman!" No one dared to pick up a stone. They could not. It was not possible. They were not without sin; they were all guilty. All, except for one man, Jesus.

The woman lay trembling at His feet, sobbing. Jesus could judge her, He had that right, but instead He wrote some words in the sand. Everyone waited – in quietness. Slowly, the sound of shuffling feet began. One by one, the religious leaders and the crowd faded into the distance, leaving the accused woman at the feet of Jesus. All was silent. There was no one left to condemn her, no men with rocks in their hands. She focused on the man who stood in front of her. Jesus turned, in kindness, to the precious woman, and looked at her. He knew her wounds, felt her shame. He touched her head and spoke with tender mercy, "Neither do I condemn you, go and sin no more."[76]

A miracle happened. There had been evidence of her actions, irrefutable guilt, upheld by several witnesses. But now she was forgiven; she was free. Free of condemnation. Free to walk without shame. No longer guilty. A fountain of intense love washed over her.

Jesus is the same yesterday, today, and forever.[77] Jesus did not come into this world to condemn or judge us, but to

---

[76] John 8:10-11
[77] Hebrews 13:8

save us.[78] He offers forgiveness, to save people from being destroyed by their guilt. Instead of death, there is life. It is a gift from Him to you and to me.

Zephaniah 3:17 – For the Lord your God is living among you. He is a mighty Saviour. He will take delight in you with gladness. With His love, he will calm all your fears. He will rejoice over you with joyful songs.

Come to Jesus. Look into His eyes, know that you are loved:
- immeasurably.
- infinitely.
- unconditionally.
- sacrificially.
- perfectly.
- in absolute delight.

SELAH - PAUSE WITH ME.

While on Earth, Jesus forgave people even before His sacrificial death had occurred. A paralytic man was brought to Jesus for healing.[79] Before Jesus healed this man physically, Jesus pronounced forgiveness of sin to him. The religious leaders of the day were furious that Jesus would dare to 'forgive' someone. That was blasphemy. They knew that only God had the right to forgive sin and they did not believe that Jesus was the Son of God. But Jesus was God and He did have the right to forgive an individual, after all, the sin was against Him. As it is with us, an offended person has the right to forgive the offender.

I marvel at some of the last words spoken by Jesus when He was hanging on the cross. He looked at those around Him

---

[78] John 3:17
[79] Luke 5:20-24

and cried out, "Father, forgive them because they don't know what they are doing."[80]

Was Jesus saying that the soldiers did not know what they were doing? The soldiers had crucified hundreds of criminals, prisoners of war and political troublemakers. That was their job. They went to work, day after day, crucifying people. That was how they earned their pay cheque. In their minds, Jesus was just another man, condemned to die.

Isaiah 53:5 – He was pierced for our rebellion, crushed for our sins. He was beaten so we could be whole, He was whipped so we could be healed.

In the last three hours that Jesus hung on the cross, darkness entombed the land. An eerie darkness. The sun hid. Nature stood silent. Jesus shouted out, "It is finished" then gave up His spirit.[81] God's love exploded. The earth shook. Rocks split apart. Tombs opened, releasing their captives.[82] In the temple, invisible hands ripped the heavy curtain that separated the holy God from mankind. It was torn from top to bottom, revealing what was inside – the Holy of Holies.

It has been a Jewish custom, for a father who had lost his beloved son, to rent his robe in anguish. He would grab his garment at the chest and tear it wide open. It was like the renting of the heavy curtain, revealing the anguish of God's heart. Such deep sorrow.

For centuries, the curtain had hung within the temple as an impenetrable shield, separating the Holy Presence of God from sinful mankind. Now that the final sacrifice had been made, the curtain was no longer necessary, removing the separation between mankind and Holy God. His heart was

---

[80]Luke 23:34
[81] John 19:30
[82] Matthew 27:51-53

visible for all to see. Open for all to enter. God's precious Son, Jesus, died to open the way for us to enter into His Presence.

Because of Jesus' death, our guilt and the blemish of sin is transformed into holiness. The stark sneering face of guilt dissipates. The mark of sin is washed clean; the crimson stain of sin becomes white as snow.[83] Guilt has been paid in full.

Romans 6:23 – For the wages of sin is death, but the free gift of God is eternal life through Christ Jesus our Lord.

Forgiveness is offered to us as a gift. It is up to you and me to accept it, to have our receipt stamped, 'PAID IN FULL'. How glorious to be free! God's plan makes it possible for us to walk with Him. There is no need to hide or to be swaddled in shame. No reason to carry the burden of guilt. We are free, free to live. Our Father God waits for us to receive His forgiveness.

JOHN'S STORY:

John came for an Inner Healing Session, overwhelmed with guilt. Hopelessness had taken reign within his mind. He was guilty and there was nothing that could undo what he had done. John had done the unforgiveable.

He had, for too long, wandered down a dark trail. He made bad decisions, and his guilt drove him to make more bad decisions, producing more guilt. Year after year, his guilt compounded, increasing its load. He wanted to stop this destructive train. He wanted to get off. But the fuel of guilt kept propelling him down that dark path. It became unbearable.

After hearing John speak of his guilt, I asked him, "Do you want to know what you can do with that guilt?"

He could feel my excitement. "Yes. Yes, please tell me!"

---

[83] Isaiah 1:18

I replied, "Guilt means that you did something wrong and it's not okay."

John wholeheartedly responded, "I know it's not okay and that's why I have guilt!"

"Jesus knows it's not okay", I said, then continued, "He knows that we all do things that are wrong. That's why He came to Earth. That's why He died, to take on our condemnation. His sacrificial blood met the requirement of our debt of sin. That's why Jesus died. He died for our guilt."

The gift of forgiveness was offered from Jesus to John. It was his to receive.

John craved for a life without guilt. He gave Jesus all his guilt and accepted Jesus' payment for his sin. He invited Jesus into his life. The huge load of heaviness was lifted. He walked out of my office with a smile on his face. It radiated joy. His heart was full of peace. He was filled with wonderment.

When John came to see me the following week, he told me that his mind kept going through all of his guilt-filled memories. He rehearsed in his mind the things that used to hold condemnation for him. But the guilt was gone! He searched every remembrance of the guilt that had held his soul captive. It was gone. He was truly free.

John told me his story of how the guilt began:
As a young child, he had no father and his alcoholic mother was always gone, either at work or a party. They moved a lot so he had no friends and was lonely. As a young boy, he wandered the streets instead of going to school. He hated school because he felt stupid. John had trouble learning because he needed glasses. His one blessing was his Grandmother.

When John was eleven years old, he accidentally bumped the wooden piano stool and broke it. Fearful, he stuck it together so no one would know. One day, when his grandmother sat on the stool, it fell apart, causing her to fall off and injure her elbow. She needed surgery. The night before her operation, she had a heart attack and died. The little boy's world fell apart. He felt so very guilty, thinking he had caused her death.

His tender little heart was crushed. The agony of losing his dear grandmother pierced him with excruciating pain and deep sorrow. He felt alone, sad, and guilty. He felt absolutely worthless. The guilt was an overwhelming heaviness. His world became lonely because nobody cared, nobody loved him. That was when John stopped caring about his life.

At age thirteen, he started drinking and, throughout his teenage years, partied with his mom. He began criminal activity. At age fifteen, he was charged with robbery. His criminal record multiplied, resulting in decades of jail time, rotting away in a cell. Life was full of devastation and nobody missed him.

Many times, he relived the memory of his mother telling him that his grandmother had died. In the memory, he ran to his bedroom and sobbed. It was then, that the humongous weight of guilt crushed him. The little boy did not know that Jesus was with him, in the midst of his pain, but now, as a grown man, he knows. When John went back to the memory, he sensed Jesus' presence with him. Jesus spoke into the depth of John's soul, telling him that is was not his fault that his beloved grandmother died. This powerful truth invaded John's soul.

John 8:32 – And you will know the truth, and the truth will set you free.

There was a 'knowing' of the truth when Jesus spoke to John, and he was set free. Great relief and joy flooded into John's heart. The blame he had felt was gone. He had no reason to numb his pain anymore. The pain was gone and his soul could breathe in quietness. There was no trace of guilt; he was free to live – free to be the amazing man that God created.

Psalm 103:12 – He has removed our sins as far from us as the east is from the west.

COLE'S STORY:

Cole was burdened with guilt. He was convicted of an act that he could not recall because he had been in a drunken stupor when it happened. The act had been committed by him and he was guilty.

I wanted Cole to understand what forgiveness looked like, so I told him a story about a person who was guilty of a crime and given six months to pay the fine. When the verdict was stated in court, a man stood up and declared that he would pay the fine. The guilty man thought it was a prank, and left with one thing in his mind, working to pay off his debt. After three months, he returned to the court cashier and handed over half of the payment, promising to pay the rest in the next three months. The court cashier looked into the books and said there was no debt owing, it had been paid – paid in full. That was when the man remembered the stranger stating that he would pay the debt. It was hard to believe, but it was true, he was free of his debt. I explained to Cole that this was exactly what Jesus had done for him. Jesus had already paid for his guilt. He was forgiven.

When I finished explaining this story to Cole, he looked at me in utter astonishment and explained that this very thing had happened to him the day before. He had gone to his probation officer to confirm his debt. He dreaded meeting with her, but knew he had to. The probation officer looked into her records and stated that he owed nothing, he had satisfied his debt by spending time in jail. Now he was free and clear of his debt. A heavy, overbearing burden had lifted. Cole had a huge smile on his face, was overjoyed, ecstatic.

He gave his guilt to Jesus and accepted the gift of forgiveness. He left my office at peace with himself and with

Jesus. He was floating on air. What a beautiful gift he had received from God.

A gift is not a gift if we have to pay for it. A gift is not a gift if we have earned it. A gift is a gift because we do not deserve it and yet it is ours because someone gives it to us, because they love us. It is our choice to receive this forgiveness. It is a gift for us to receive. Jesus did this for us – me and you.

A gift of love is a token of affection and appreciation. When a gift is received, there is a fullness of love. Forgiveness is a gift to be received. Forgiveness cannot be earned and it is not deserved. It is free and it is life-giving.

We cannot earn forgiveness by trying to be good. Nothing can excuse us of our guilt. We can spend the rest of our lives trying to correct what we have done, or should have done, but the stain of sin remains. When we receive God's forgiveness, the consequences of our actions are still present but the guilt is gone. Jesus gave His life so that we can receive forgiveness of our sins.

Isaiah 1:18 – "Come now, let's settle this," says the Lord. "Though your sins are like scarlet, I will make them as white as snow. Though they are red like crimson, I will make them as white as wool."

At times, it is hard for us to receive forgiveness, not understanding how it is possible. We do not deserve the love of Jesus dying for us. Yet, the truth is, Jesus welcomes us into His presence.

In historical times, no one entered the presence of the king without being invited. The king held the power of life and death in his hands. His words were final. The king's power was revered, though not always respected.

In the Old Testament, there was one woman who dared to come into the king's presence without being summoned.

84

She was not an ordinary woman; she was his wife. But even her position did not guarantee her safety. It was possible that he might have moved on to another woman. She had no idea if she would be alive after her daring appearance. No one entered the king's presence without being summoned – unless that person was already threatened with death. That was the case of Queen Esther.

Her appearance was planned. After many days of fasting and prayer, she dressed in royal attire and entered the throne room, uninvited. From the corner of her eye – she watched the hand that held the scepter, the object that dictated whether she would live or die. She bowed in reverence.

The king lifted his scepter and gently asked what it was that she wanted. The Queen's life was spared. She had been forgiven for appearing without being summoned. She was granted life.

God is not like an earthly king. Though God is to be revered above all else. He holds out His scepter to us – continuously. It is the object of powerful grace, extended to us because of the death of His Son, Jesus, who forgave our sin. We are accepted into His presence – always, anytime. Without guilt. Without condemnation.

God encourages us to come boldly into heaven's most Holy Place. We have that privilege because of the blood of Jesus. We are invited to come into the presence of God with sincere hearts, fully trusting Him. Christ's blood has washed away our guilt. The invitation stands today for each of us to enter into Jesus' presence. Come, you are invited into the presence of God. The invitation has your personal name on it.

In the New Testament, a new term is introduced regarding our God, the King. It speaks to us about our 'Abba Father'.[84] Abba is a term of endearment between child and father. Papa. It is a term that welcomes the child to come and

---

[84] Galatians 4:6

sit on his knee. To be held. To have his little body wrapped up in delightful embrace. Perhaps receive a tickle or a beard rub. Maybe a touching of his chin, a kiss on the nose. Perhaps the father's fingers playing with the child's hair. Perhaps a hand of blessing upon their head. That is the heart of our Papa Father towards us, His children.

Invite God's love into your heart and let it flow. It will cleanse your every sin. Give Him permission to fill the void in your heart. It will drive out the darkness, the heaviness of guilt, and shame. Let it flow into the depths of your soul. Let Him restore you. His sceptre of forgiveness is extended to you without condemnation. It is His invitation for you to come into His presence. His desire is to have you close, to hold you, to fill you with life – His life.

PRAYER: – Freedom from guilt; receiving forgiveness
My dear Papa Father. I have trouble comprehending that you love me so very much and yet I choose to believe that you really do. Thank you, dear Father, for sending your Son, Jesus, and thank you, Jesus, for being willing to endure all that suffering for me. You understand the depth of my pain. Thank you for making the way of peace for me. I am so very guilty of (name your sin). I know what I did was wrong and that's why I need your forgiveness. I don't want to carry this heavy burden of guilt any longer. It's too heavy. I give it to you, all of it – and I receive your forgiveness. Cleanse me of my sins. I open my heart for You to wash me clean. Thank you for dying for me, for paying the price of my sin. Thank you for your forgiveness. Thank you for your amazing gift to me. I receive your Holy Spirit. Fill me with your peace. In the name of Jesus, Amen.

See how very much our Father loves us,
for He calls us His children,
and that is what we are!
- I John 3:1

REFLECTIONS: Chapter 6 – Forgiven!

1. What are the parallels between offering sacrifices in the Old Testament and the death of Jesus?
2. How is it possible to be forgiven?
3. What did Jesus think of the adulterous woman? How would you have acted towards her?
4. Why would Jesus forgive her when she was guilty?
5. What does it mean to be forgiven?
6. Jesus offers you forgiveness. It is yours, His gift to you.
7. Give Him all your guilt. Let Him cleanse you of your sin and fill your heart with His love.
8. What does it look like for Him to be your Abba Father?

Notes & Journaling:

_____

_____

_____

_____

_____

_____

_____

Chapter 7

Forgiving Others, Forgiving One's Self

Grace and mercy are amazing! They are beautiful gifts – undeserved. Unearned. Given as a token of kindness.

Jesus spoke a story in Matthew 18, which demonstrated grace and mercy at its greatest. This illustration was about a king who decided to bring his receivables up to date. It was discovered that one of his servants owed him millions of dollars. The servant was brought before the king. It was time to pay. It was time to give back to the king what had been borrowed. But the servant could not pay the debt.

The king ordered the man to be sold – alongside his wife and children – to pay the debt. The servant flung himself down before the king. He begged for more time to pay back the money, beseeching mercy for himself and his family.

The king looked at him, heard the servant's wailing. His heart softened, became tender and pliable. He felt pity for the servant's desperate state. The king decided to forgive the debt – all of it, to set the man and his family free.

That deep kindness is called grace. The servant had borrowed the money and owed the debt of millions of dollars. The king deserved to be paid back; the money was legally his. But the king erased the debt. Wiped it clean. The servant accepted the grace and left. No more debt. Amazing.

Luke 7 reveals a story of a woman who came to Jesus while He was visiting another house. She came, profusely thanking Him for His grace towards her, gifting Him with a bottle of rare, expensive perfume which she poured on Jesus' feet. People, witnessing this, were upset to see the waste of such a precious commodity. She could have sold it and given the money to the poor. But Jesus spoke, announcing that her behaviour was an act of intense tenderness and deep love for Him. Her sin had been great and she was forgiven. She accepted God's grace, with deep gratitude. Jesus stated that people who have been forgiven much, will love much in return.[85]

Such gratefulness should have been within the servant who was forgiven his large debt. But after the servant left the king, he sought a man who owed him money. A few thousand dollars, a small amount by comparison to the millions that he had just been forgiven. He demanded it to be paid, instantly. When the man could not pay, he was thrown into jail. The other servants could not believe it and informed the King of what he had done. The King reacted in fury, ordering the previously absolved man into his presence. He called him evil, and sent him to prison, to be tortured – forever. Without mercy.

BRIAN'S STORY:

When Brian came to an Inner Healing Session, his words spewed hatred for his father. Brian was the youngest of five boys. One day, the family went on holidays, stopped at a gas station, filled up the car with gas and proceeded down the road. Brian was accidentally left behind. His heart was crushed. He felt worthless and forgotten. Brian sat down on a bench, filled with fear. His anger mounted. When the family returned to pick him up, fifteen minutes later, he was reprimanded – it was his fault for being left behind.

Going back into the memory, Brian sensed that Jesus was beside him on the bench, protecting him from anyone who might have wanted to kidnap him. But Brian was vehemently angry at his dad, for forgetting him those fifteen

---

[85] Luke 7:47

minutes. For decades he held on to that anger and could not forgive his dad.

I asked Jesus if He had anything to say to Brian, in his state of unforgiveness and anger. Brian was quiet. After a minute, he looked at me, dumbfounded. Yes, his dad had forgotten him for fifteen minutes, but Brian had abandoned his own son for nine months during his time of drug use. He was stunned. He saw the difference between his neglect over the 393,120 minutes (nine months) compared to the 15 minutes his father had forgotten him. He was astonished. Brian realized that his offense was so much greater than what his father had done to him.

If Brian did not forgive, then he could not be forgiven. Brian gave God his anger towards his dad. By forgiving his dad, Brian was able to forgive himself. When he received God's forgiveness, the heaviness was lifted from his being. He was now free to be the amazing man that God created him to be – without anger, without guilt.

Matthew 6:14-15 – If you forgive those who sin against you, your heavenly Father will forgive you. But if you refuse to forgive others, your Father will not forgive your sins.

While on the cross, Jesus cried out, "Father, forgive them, for they don't know what they are doing."[86] During His excruciating pain, within His body, mind, soul, and spirit, He forgave:
- those who were gambling for his clothes.[87]
- the man on the next cross who was jeering Jesus' power.[88]
- the religious leaders who were condemning Him for something He did not do.[89]

---

[86] Luke 23:34
[87] John 19:23-24
[88] Matthew 27:44
[89] Matthew 27:41-43

- the crowds who previously hailed Him as their 'Saviour' were now verbally sneering at Him, mocking Him.[90]
- the soldiers who crucified Him.

He had been whipped severely, then nailed to a cross, yet He had no violent words on His lips. His eyes filled with compassion. The soldiers saw Him as only another man being crucified; one man in a long line of crosses.

A plaque had been placed above His head on the cross, containing the words: 'King of the Jews'. Jesus knew He was the Son of God. He knew His mission was to die on behalf of all mankind, absolving all guilt. The soldiers did not know this. It was God's plan for them to crucify Jesus. They were fulfilling prophesy, not knowing they had just killed the Son of God, the One who had created them. The man they had nailed on the cross was dying so their sins could be forgiven.

When Jesus died, the earth shook. The officers and soldiers were terrified, for they realized they had murdered the Son of God.[91] The centurion exclaimed that surely this man was innocent. He worshipped God.[92] But it was too late to change what had already been done. Jesus had died. He had forgiven the soldiers and did not hold them accountable for his death. What a merciful God we have.

Sin is more than visible actions. Sin can be lack of action. Sin can be words or lack of them. It can be hiding something, speaking part-truth. Temptation begins in the mind: we have a choice as to what we do with the temptation. Entertain it, give it power, or drive it out. God is aware of what is happening in our mind. Our thoughts are evident to Him. If you claim to have no sin, God says that you are only fooling yourself.[93] Each of us are guilty of sin. We need to forgive as God forgives us.

---

[90] Mark 15:29-30
[91] Matthew 27:54
[92] Luke 23:47
[93] 1 John 1:8

Ephesians 4:32 - Be kind to each other, tender-hearted, forgiving one another, just as God, through Christ, has forgiven you.

Forgive them. He died for you and He also died for those who treated you unjustly. Since He forgave you, you need to forgive others. Forgiving is more than thinking that you should forgive, it is more than saying it. It must come from your heart, and your actions.

MY STORY:

Many years ago, on a cold and snowy November day, I was invited to meet two women to discuss the prospect of speaking at a ladies' function. I had previously written out my speech and sent it to them so that we could discuss it. When we met, the women spoke harshly to me about my proposed talk. I began to cry; my soul was crushed.

We parted. They left, driving into a winter storm. I sat in my vehicle, my soul heaving. I cried out to God and forgave them. It was wrong what they had done, and that is why I forgave them. I left them in God's hands. Days later, I learned that they were both killed in a head on collision just after they left me. My first reaction was "I'm so thankful that I forgave them!" I could not share this incident with anyone for many years because it impacted me so deeply.

When we forgive others, their sins are forgiven because we choose to forgive them. Jesus said that when we are in Christ, we do have authority in His name. We have the power and the privilege to release the grace of God upon those who have trespassed us. Be it a betrayal, a spoken word, or something that was not done. We hold the key of forgiveness. It is up to us to forgive. We have the privilege of liberating ourselves and also the offender, to forgive them just as Jesus has forgiven us. As we gift forgiveness to our offender, we release heaven's favour upon them and we are blessed with peace deeply within us. We put them in God's hands; He is the One who deals with them. God is just; He is also compassionate. He knows what to do with them. We choose to trust Him with them and are free to live.

Forgiveness is essential. It is crucial to living, taking a weight off our shoulders. Forgiveness does not mean that the offense is okay. When anyone hurts you, they are hurting God. Anyone who harms you, harms God's most precious possession.[94] God offers forgiveness to them and so must we. We need to forgive.

Forgiveness does not mean that you have to trust that person. Forgiveness is between you and God, while trust is between you and the individual. Forgiveness is a gift while trust is earned. God commands us to forgive; He does not command us to trust. He alone is absolutely trustworthy.

THOMAS' STORY:
Thomas was younger than his two brothers, who were six and eight years older than himself. He felt lonely, like an only child. When he was four years old, his mom and dad separated and fought for custody of their three sons. His mom won the court case – then weeks later, told their father to come for the three boys, otherwise she would adopt them out. She did not want them anymore. The brothers went to live with their dad. Thomas was furious with his mother and called her by her first name, his way of totally disowning her, with no possibility of forgiving her. He was determined that she did not deserve his forgiveness. She had done the unforgiveable; the betrayal of a mom rejecting her child.

Thomas came to the Inner Healing Sessions and kept delaying forgiveness of his mom. He declared that he did not have to go back to his boyhood memories. Thomas' pain was too great to face, nor was he ready to forgive his mother. He

---

[94] Matthew 18:22

94

was stuck in his pain. Jesus was waiting for him to come to Him with his anger. Jesus understood. He too had been betrayed.

Before Thomas left the rehabilitation program, he received news from his doctor that his liver was in critical condition, due to excessive use of alcohol. Not willing to forgive his mother, his agony went with him wherever he went. He was stuck in his anger.

When you choose not to forgive someone, they win. You give them power; they are still tormenting you. Their cruel words and actions replay in your mind. Your emotions are controlled by them; you are allowing them to keep abusing you. You still feel the pain. Forgive them and put them in God's hands to deal with. It will free you from their clutches. You will be free to live, to be the person that God created you to be.

Jesus was asked by his disciple, Peter, "How often should I forgive someone? Seven times?"

Jesus replied, "Not seven times but seventy times seven times."[95] That is literally 490 times! His point was: there is no limit when it comes to forgiving someone. We must forgive no matter what – always, all the time, without counting the number of times.

We can forgive someone:
- without telling them.
- when they are not sorry.
- even though they keep doing it.
- who has already died.

Forgiveness is between God and us. It is a choice of our heart.

In the story regarding the king bringing judgement upon the ungrateful servant, he set the secondary servant free while

---

[95] Matthew 18:22

the ungrateful one was put into jail to be tortured. God is a just God and asks us to forgive just as He forgives us. He is justified in stating that if we do not forgive others, then He will not forgive us.

Unforgiveness poisons us. It is a darkness that invades our soul; a heavy weight entering our being. We are warned about bitterness taking root and overtaking our soul.

Hebrews 12:15 – Look after each other so that none of you fails to receive the grace of God. Watch out that no poisonous root of bitterness grows up to trouble you, corrupting many.

During the facilitation of Inner Healing Sessions, I have discovered that the unforgiving person often becomes like the offender, when they do not forgive. By not forgiving those who have trespassed, they allow the cycle of destruction to continue. God knows that we need to forgive and that is why He commands us to do so.

PRAYER: to Forgive Others
Dear Papa God. Thank you for dying for me. I know that You forgave me and so I choose to forgive (person/s) for (the offense). It was wrong what he/she did to me. Very wrong. I have forgiven them because you have forgiven me, I choose to forgive them. They really didn't know what they were doing. I release them from their guilt towards me and I put them into your hands for you to deal with. Thank you for the gift of forgiving me and I extend this gift of forgiveness to them. Fill me with your peace and joy. In the name of Jesus, Amen.

When we are disappointed with ourselves, our guilt may disable us to forgive ourselves. We feel that we need to be punished. Guilt is a heavy burden; it restricts life. Guilt suffocates. Guilt brings darkness and hopelessness. It drives unhealthy behaviour and tries to compensate for the wrong. Our souls cry out in anguish. We may have failed others, ourselves, or God, through what we have done, said or did not do. We need to forgive ourselves.

Jesus beseeched His Father in Luke 23:34: "Father forgive them, for they don't know what they are doing." You can forgive yourself because you did not know what you were doing. Even if you intended to do it, you did not understand the whole picture, did not realize the consequences. Choose to forgive yourself.

Are you guilty? Is it true guilt? If so, bring your guilt to Jesus. He died to pay for your guilt. Receive His forgiveness. If it is false guilt, then let it go.

BELINDA'S STORY:

Belinda had been using drugs. The gangs she was involved with, controlled her and her son. One day her three-year-old son took two pills of oxycodone that had been left on the table, potency enough to kill. Her son turned blue; he was dying. The ambulance was called; Belinda was terrified. It was the worst possible nightmare – and she was responsible.

When going back into the memory, Belinda saw Jesus praying over them, touching her son's forehead. He was witnessing the paramedics accidentally breaking the boy's ribs while administering CPR. Her son's pulse was activated and he began to breathe. It was a miracle. After two weeks in the hospital, he recovered.

Belinda could not carry her guilt any longer, it was too heavy. She had not given the pills to her son but she was guilty for not watching over him and protecting him. False and true guilt feel the same but are dealt with in different ways. Belinda gave her true guilt to God for not being a good mom and received Jesus' forgiveness, then forgave herself. She released the false guilt that she nearly killed her son. False guilt was not hers to carry. She was now free to live. The guilt was gone.

PRAYER: to Forgive Self

Dear Papa God. Thank you for sending Jesus to Earth to die on the cross for my wrongs. I receive your forgiveness for what I did/didn't do. I didn't realize what I was doing but it was wrong. Thank you for forgiving me for (name it). And I choose to forgive myself. I give you my guilt. Thank you, Jesus, for dying for it and setting me free!

SHAME:

One of guilt's fellow companions is shame. Shame becomes part of one's identity, as if a label has been stamped upon one's being. Shame is placed upon children by inflicting physical or sexual abuse, or through words. The child feels compelled to wear the heavy coat of shame. Once shame is accepted by the child, it accumulates in mass, suffocating their inner being. Their head hangs low. They cannot stand tall.

Jesus knows the fullness of shame and dying as a criminal. Men who were crucified were often naked, vulnerable for any passerby to ridicule them, making sport of them. Everyone in the city of Jerusalem knew what had happened to Jesus, He was on display, the talk of the city. Jesus knows what shame feels like. He took our shame upon Himself; we do not have to carry it. We have a choice: We can keep wearing it, or give it to Jesus.

VICTORIA'S STORY:

Victoria felt shame. It was grotesque and ugly; it made her feel hideous. In her Inner Healing Session, she relived the shame and followed it back to where it had begun, at age seven, when she was raped by her step-dad. Her mom blamed Victoria for it happening. Victoria had tried to wash off her dirtiness by having a shower, but she could not get rid of it.

She felt there was an air bubble in her chest filled with emptiness, guilt, sadness and hopelessness.

When I asked her if she could sense Jesus in the memory, she said He was up in the sky, watching over her. She wanted Him to hug her and keep her safe. Jesus spoke to her, told her she was loved, was strong, that it was not her fault. He told her that He was the One who would cleanse her. Her chest was filled with His love and comfort. She was a child of God, the one true King. Victoria said that it felt like a bunch of angels were around her, their wings making her feel warm, safe and loved. Jesus took her shame and gave her love, hope and forgiveness.

In another of Victoria's memories, she was supposed to watch her little brother in the bathtub. But he slipped and fell. She felt guilty and more shame was heaped upon her. It was her fault. Her mom whipped her with a belt. It was extremely painful. She felt helpless, worthless, alone and lost.

In the memory, she sensed Jesus was with her in the bathroom. He touched her face gently and said that it was not her fault. It was an accident. He told her that He knew what it felt like to be beaten. He too had been whipped. Jesus went on to say that her mom felt trapped, that she did not know how to ask for help.

Victoria made a list of things that she needed to forgive her mom for, then forgave her because she did not know what she was doing. She placed her mom in God's hands. She was free from the shame and false guilt. She no longer had to carry the sins of her mother.

PRAYER: Taking off the Coat of Shame
I am wearing this sickening coat of shame. It feels so disgusting. It was put on me when (recall the incident when it was put on you). I choose to forgive (name the person/s) for putting it on me. It was so wrong what they did and I choose to forgive them. Jesus, I give you this ugly coat of shame. I don't want to wear

it anymore. It's all yours. Clothe me in your purity. Thank you that I can be free to love myself. You have made me whole!

Sometimes, a hideous act is forced upon a child, making them feel shameful. This is called false guilt. Over time, this despicable act, becomes acceptable and the person willingly participates in it – making it true guilt.

- True guilt is confessed to God and forgiveness is received.
- False guilt is given to God, and forgiveness is given to the offender.

Forgiving others is commanded by God for a very good reason. God has forgiven us; therefore, we must forgive others. Forgiveness is the decision to place the offender into God's hands and set them free from our minds. We release the person of their guilt; they do not owe us anything anymore. They are accountable to God now. When we forgive, we are filled with His peace. Thank you, dear Jesus for dying for us. Thank you for forgiving us and giving us the courage and power to forgive others.

Forgive us our sins, as we have forgiven those who sin against us.
– Matthew 6:12

REFLECTIONS: Chapter 7 – Forgiving others, Forgiving self

1. What is grace?
2. What makes it hard to forgive someone?
3. What happens when I forgive someone?
4. What is the difference between forgiving and trusting?
5. How does unforgiveness affect us?
6. Who do I need to forgive?
   - Choose to release that person from the offense.
   - Put that person into God's hands.
   - Trust God that He will deal with that person.
7. How are forgiveness and shame connected?
8. Is there anything that I need to forgive myself for?

Notes & Journaling:

_____

_____

_____

_____

_____

_____

_____

_____

_____

_____

_____

_____

_____

_____

_____

_____

Chapter 8

The Wall of Anger

Thirteen-year-old Cari was walking down a country road, going to a church carnival. She was full of excitement, anticipation, and delight. It was a normal day in May, 1980. The sun was shining and the birds were busy making their nests when it happened – tragedy struck from behind. A drunk driver smashed into the teenager – then drove away. It was a hit and run. Cari's body was thrown one hundred and twenty-five feet. Mutilated. Her organs were so severely damaged that they were not functional enough to donate.[96] Cari's mom, Candy Lightner, was angry.

Cari no longer smiled. Her legs were limp and still. Her eyes lifeless. Cari had died. Candy's soul was shattered.

The driver had been released on bail only two days before Cari's death. The previous charge: drunk driving. Cari's death was his fifth offense in four years.[97] Candy found out that the drunk driver would probably not spend any time in jail. She was furious.

Anger is a part of our makeup, for we are created in the image of God. Anger is the result of a perceived injustice, and we should be angry. Every injustice is wrong. Even a small child knows when something is not right. We are born with the insight of justice. Nobody needs to teach us, we just know. Injustice shapes our understanding and beliefs, affecting who we are, who we think God is, and what we do with our lives.

---

[96] Alcohol: Problems and solutions, Candy Lightner (Candace Lightner): Founder of MADD, n.d., alcoholproblemsandsolutions.org
[97] Ibid.

Learned behaviours affect how we deal with injustice. Many times, we get angry and do not consider its affect.

Anger is powerful. It is a secondary emotion, trying to cover up the raw feelings beneath it. The painful belief beneath it is side-stepped when anger takes over.

MICHAELS' STORY:

When Michael came for an Inner Healing Session, he was angry at himself. As a little boy, he was reprimanded for singing so vigorously one morning at school. His little soul boisterously bellowed out the melody. The children began to snicker, then burst into howls of laughter. The teacher joined in the ridicule of the little boy's lusty expression of delightful singing. Michael was mortified. He became the laughing stock of the class, feeling worthless. I asked him why he was angry at himself. He harshly judged himself for allowing the possibility of being mocked and scorned, before all his classmates and his teacher. The little boy chided himself, "Why did I sing so loudly?"

Michael was angry that he was not perfect, that he was not able to sing perfectly. Michael's deep pain was an immobilizing woundedness. We explored further to discover his belief of worthlessness. In going back to the memory, Michael saw Jesus beside him; He knew what to say – "I love your heart, keep singing. It makes you beautiful." Now there was no reason to keep the anger.

A wall of anger can be built for many reasons. It:
- protects oneself from feeling raw, painful emotions.
- displays power and dominance.
- keeps others from igniting painful memories.
- becomes the boundary marker of 'no trespassing', keeping certain people out of your life.
- gives energy to motivate and accomplish tasks.

- determines who is to blame.
- is used for revenge.
- controls people and situations.

Anger is normal. Nowhere in the Bible does it say that anger is wrong. In the Old Testament, God got angry. Jesus got angry while He was on the earth. But God does say that we need to deal with the anger, do something with it, do not keep it - do not erect a wall of anger.

Ephesians 4:26-27 – Don't sin by letting anger control you. Don't let the sun go down while you are still angry, for anger gives a foothold to the devil.

Anger has many faces:
- revenge, hate
- wrath and rage
- malice
- impatience, frustration, irritation
- stone silence, non-responsive behaviour
- depression

Our bodies are not designed to keep anger. The chemical reaction of anger within our brain is the same as it is for fear; both are destructive to the body. Dr. Caroline Leaf, a neuroscientist, stated that toxic emotions cause the electrical chemical processes to be over-activated within the brain. If anger is kept, chemicals continuously flood the synapse through which electrical impulses are passed from one nerve cell to another. This non-stop pouring into the gap causes the ends of the nerve cells, the dendrites, to become 'poisoned' and they wither into uselessness. The brain cannot function. This inflammation within the brain can be seen on a brain scan as black clouds. The good news is that with the cessation of this abnormal flow of neurotransmitters, the nerve endings can regain health.[98]

Injustice disturbs us, and it should. We become angry for a good reason.

OUTCOMES OF ANGER:

1. Helplessness and Depression

When anger is not acknowledged, it is covered up, pushed down, denied. There is a sense of being trapped and the energy of anger crushes life, creating a heavy millstone in the core of one's being. The dark cloud of heaviness suffocates the soul.

JACK'S STORY:

Jack had a golden childhood; he could charm everyone. As a teenager, he loved to party and was voted King of the high-school prom. He was every girl's dream. Jack had the ability to woo any woman. He thought of women as trophies he had conquered. There were many. It felt great to have power and control. After leaving school, Jack committed to a steady girlfriend. After two years, she broke off the relationship and he fell into a deep depression. She was the first of many girlfriends who had abandoned him. He got into a number of relationships and after every breakup, Jack fell more deeply into depression. He felt helpless. His pain of abandonment was guarded by his anger, he felt helpless and lost hope. Jack had fallen into sustained anger.

2. Positive Action

When Cari was killed by a drunk driver, her mother, Candace Lightner, promised herself that her daughter's death would count for something positive. Instead of being consumed by

---

[98] Coastal Church Podcast, The Dirty Dozen by Dr. Caroline Leaf, www.coastalchurch.org listened to on Jan.23,2016

anger, Lightner channeled her emotions by starting MADD (Mothers Against Drunk Driving).

The group had two goals:
- raise public awareness surrounding the serious nature of drunk driving
- promote tougher legislation against the crime

Lightner and her organization worked tirelessly resulting in over 400 drunk driving laws being passed across the USA.[99] Its huge impact was, and is, the reduction of traffic crashes, therefore saving many lives.

While anger can drive us to take positive action, holding on to anger is poison within our souls. Jesus was angry and took the whip through the temple to clear the marketplace. But He did not stay angry. He went out and healed people, touched people compassionately and had mercy upon broken hearts. His anger did not stay in His heart. King David wrote in one of his Psalms that God's anger is short-lived.

Psalm 30:5- God's anger lasts only a moment but His favour lasts a lifetime

Kept anger is not a positive emotion, it is damaging. Kept anger results in bitterness which in turn causes an ever-expanding path of darkness. The soul becomes infected. Anger is normal, but when allowed to keep us hostage, the soul is weakened and bitterness takes over.

3. Revenge

Anger is used to execute justice, with no holds barred. Rage takes over. Revenge becomes a powerful destructive force against the offender. In Judges 15, Samson was burning with

---

[99] Alcohol: Problems and solutions, Candy Lightner (Candace Lightner): Founder of MADD, n.d., alcoholproblemsandsolutions.org

anger over the fact that his wife was given to another man. He was furious. He had a good reason to be angry. He said: "I have a right to get even." "I won't stop until I get revenge on you." "I merely did to them what they did to me."

Romans 12:19 – Dear friends, never take revenge. Leave that to the righteous anger of God. For the Scriptures say, "I will take revenge; I will pay them back," says the Lord.

CAIN'S STORY:

Anger has been present since the beginning of mankind. In Genesis 4, we discover God's thoughts, regarding the first-time anger was mentioned in the Bible. Cain was furious at his brother, because Abel's sacrifice was acceptable to God but his was not. Cain harboured intense fury towards Abel.

I love reading about God's response to Cain's anger. When God addressed Cain, God did not lecture Cain for being angry. God has never reprimanded mankind for getting angry. Instead, God asked Cain why he was furious.

Cain's sacrifice had been rejected, but it was not Abel's fault. Cain's mind dwelt on the injustice. He deflected his anger onto his brother, instead of being angry at God. But God knew about his anger. God invited Cain to talk to Him about his perceived injustice. Anger kept Cain from listening.

Genesis 4:6-7 – "Why are you so angry?" the Lord asked Cain. "You will be accepted if you do what is right. But if you refuse to do what is right, then watch out. Sin is crouching at the door, eager to control you. But you must subdue it and be its master."

God alerted Cain to be careful, be attentive, because sin was crouching at the door of his heart, waiting to control and destroy him.[100] This was a warning from God. The Bible talks about Satan being like a roaring lion, seeking someone to devour.[101] In the dry season, a lion's roar can be heard up to 3 miles (5 km) and when the air is moist his roar travels as far as 5-6 miles (8-10 km).[102] But when the lion is stalking, he is quiet.

When I was in Kenya, I went on a safari, admiring the amazing African animals. A lioness was trudging alongside our road. She looked depressed and forlorn. She veered off into the grassland. It just so happened that a warthog was sprinting swiftly in the same direction as the lioness; their paths were about to intersect, neither were aware of each other. Then all of a sudden, the lioness saw the warthog and stopped. Very carefully and stealthily, it snuck towards the path of the warthog. Whenever the warthog stopped to look around, the lioness stopped too. At just the right moment, when the lioness was close enough, it sprang out and seized the warthog. After a short struggle, the lioness enjoyed her meal.

This is what God was speaking about when He warned us to be careful. The warthog was too busy running. He did not notice the lioness until it was too late. When anger is given a crack in the door of one's soul, it lunges right into the midst of one's being and takes over. It is a powerful force and that is why God warned Cain to do what was right. Sin was crouching at the door waiting to devour.

Cain's choices:
- to subdue the anger and be its master
- let anger be master over him.

Psalm 37:8 – Stop being angry! Turn from your rage! Do not lose your temper – it only leads to harm.

---

[100] Genesis 4:6-7
[101] 1 Peter 5:8
[102] Jonathan and Angela Scott, Safari Guide to East African Animals, (p.56), 1977, Kensta

There was a period of time, between Cain's birth of anger and what happened as a result. The story goes on to say that 'one day' Cain suggested to his brother Abel to go into the field. The field was Cain's territory, and the pasture was Abel's. While in the field, Cain killed his brother, Abel.[103]

God asked Cain where his brother was. God knew, but was giving Cain the opportunity of owning his actions and repenting, confessing what he had done. But Cain's response was irresponsible. He was flippant with God, casting aside any responsibility for what he had done. Anger does that. It justifies destructive behaviour. It takes no blame, but rather blames the one who made them angry. God called him on it. Cain was responsible for what he had done.

There are always consequences when keeping anger. For Cain, God stated that the ground would no longer produce good crops for him. The area that Cain excelled as a farmer, was now going to be non-productive. The blessing of God was withdrawn, all because of Cain's anger. When it was known that Cain had murdered his brother, Cain feared he would be killed by someone. In God's compassion, He placed a mark on Cain to warn anyone who would dare to destroy him.[104] Cain lived his life, with his wife and family – but he left God's presence.

Anger separates us from God and also other people. Anger causes arguments[105] and mistakes[106], causes foolish things to happen.[107] An angry person starts fights; a hot-tempered person commits all kinds of sin.[108] Angry people can be unpredictable and dangerous, making us feel unsafe. We try to avoid conflict, from being their target.

---

[103] Genesis 4:8
[104] Genesis 4:15
[105] Proverbs 15:18
[106] Proverbs 14:29
[107] Proverbs 14:17
[108] Proverbs 29:22

Sometimes anger is drawn to anger – people of like-mind, making the injustice increase in power. The sin of keeping the anger is no longer crouching behind the door. Anger had been welcomed into the party. The merrymaking becomes chaotic and brings demolition. Anger takes control and dictates the destruction of lives.

Proverbs 22:24-25 – Don't befriend angry people or associate with hot-tempered people, or you will learn to be like them and endanger your soul.

Both suppression of anger and projecting it onto others, brings destruction. Follow anger back to the first time it was allowed to stay. That memory is where one's anger needs to be dealt with.

DANIKA'S STORY:

Danika had asked her friend to take care of her treasured dog while she was gone. When Danika got back, she discovered that her friend had abandoned her dog for five days without food or water. Anger spewed from Danika. She felt betrayed and had a deep rage well up inside of her.

I met with Danika for an Inner Healing Session and asked her to remember the very first time she got angry. A memory from age eight came to her mind, when her sister kept picking on her. One day she became so angry that she picked up the phone and hit her sister with it. She felt powerful instead of helpless. During the session, Danika had to leave the room. Reliving the past, made her angry. She returned calmer, and stated that she did not want anger to control her anymore. She gave her anger to Jesus. She placed her friend, the one who neglected her dog, into God's hands so He could deal with her. Jesus became her new bodyguard and the blood of Jesus cleansed her heart. When she left the room at the end of the session, she was flooded with peace.

111

REASONS WHY ANGER STAYS:

Some people have harboured intense anger for decades. There are reasons why we may want anger to stay:

1. Anger becomes our bodyguard.

When anger is allowed to be our bodyguard, it protects us from feeling the pain. But it takes over our life and controls our activities. It is like a person coming to your door and you allow them to come in for a few days. But pretty soon this person moves in their stuff, starts rearranging your place, dictates what foods you eat and what you can do. It is this guest in your house who determines who is allowed to visit. Anger takes over your 'house'. You have allowed it to become a permanent resident of your life and control you.

Anger becomes a shield from experiencing emotional suffering. Candy Lightner, had been 'unstoppable' in proclaiming the injustice of drunk driving and it replaced the grieving of her precious child. All else in life took second place to her campaign of injustice, MADD. In 1990, Lightner wrote a book, *Giving Sorrow Words*, where she talked of her journey, of working through her grief after five and a half years of ignoring it.[109] Anger had protected her from feeling the deep pain surrounding the death of her daughter.

Two months after my own daughter died, I woke one morning feeling angry. I was angry at God. I had questions:

- Why did He let her die this time, when all the other times, she regained her health?
- Why did He cause her to be born blind and have cerebral palsy resulting in such a difficult life?
- And why, after all my prayers for her healing, did she die anyway?

God did not answer any of my questions but asked me, "Why do you keep the anger?" I had good reason to be angry. But I

---

[109] Your Dictionary, Candy Lightner Facts, n.d., biography.yourdictionary.com

had a choice. It was up to me whether I wanted to keep this anger or let it go. I admitted to God that it felt much better to feel anger than to feel the pain of losing my daughter, that I would never see her on Earth again. Feeling anger protected me from feeling the deep pain.

I realized that the pain would stay forever if I did not face it. I would be stuck in the anger – until I allowed myself to go through the intense grief of loss. With or without anger, my daughter would never be on this earth with me again. I decided to give my anger to Jesus and I asked Him to walk with me through the grief. Jesus held me, as my sorrow bore down upon me. He understood my pain and carried me through it. My soul was, and still is, soothed by Him.

When anger becomes our bodyguard, it protects us from feeling the pain but it slowly poisons us inside. Anger protects us, but in a destructive way.

There are three options when it comes to dealing with our pain:

- Be crushed by the pain.
- Allow the destructive bodyguard of anger to protect us from feeling the pain.
- 'Fire' anger as our bodyguard and 'hire' the absolute perfect bodyguard of Jesus.

When Jesus is allowed to guard our heart, He brings healing. He knows everything that is going on just like a good bodyguard should. The beautiful first verse of Psalm 91 states that those who live in the shelter of the Most High will find rest in the shadow of the Almighty. It goes on to say that God alone is our refuge, our place of safety. He understands and comforts us. He adores us. He gave His life so we can heal. He is our Healer.

Psalm 28:7 - The Lord is my strength and shield; I will trust Him with all my heart.

Serenity is not possible when anger is present. Jesus knows about the injustice that you have suffered; He understands. He knows what it feels like to be:

- betrayed by a best friend.
- abandoned by those who say they love you.
- rejected by those who have authority over you.
- humiliated and mocked by those surrounding you.

He knows deep pain and He loves you. Let Him be your bodyguard and bring healing into your life. You do not need anger to protect yourself. Jesus is right beside you.

JAMIES' STORY:

Jamie's anger had worn her out. At age eight, her brother beat her, and pinned her to the ground. She could not breathe and her father laughed at her. This little girl felt worthless and weak, so vulnerable; there was nobody to protect her. She was alone. This made her very sad. She became angry at God for not caring about her.

Jamie was angry at her dad. That anger protected her from feeling the pain of being unloved. Jesus tried to reach her but the anger was in the way. She wanted her dad to be hurt. Her dad needed to pay for what he had done to her, for not protecting her, not loving her. Jesus told her that He was stronger than her anger and asked her to trust Him. He loved everyone, even her dad.

Then Jamie visualized Jesus dying on the cross, telling her that He loved her. Love meant that He wanted to be with her without any expectations. Finally, she opened her heart to Him and asked Him to come in.

She was no longer beaten and pinned to the ground; Jesus was holding her. She felt warm and comforted, Jesus was smiling at her. She felt safe and trusted Him. When Jamie

114

went back to the memory, there was no tension, no anger, no fear. It was just a memory - with no pain.

2. Anger within us tries to hold someone accountable.

When we give our anger to God, it does not mean that the offense was okay. We have a sense that, if we release our anger, the person gets away with the injustice. But justice can never be carried out by you; nothing can undo what was done or not done, that is why you need to give it to God. He knows what to do with it; He is a just God.

Anger keeps you tied to the offender in a destructive way. When you are angry at someone, you give them power in determining what you are thinking, what you say, and what you do. This makes you angrier because they made you do it. Blame justifies you in keeping your anger.

Anger, when given to God, means that He will take care of the injustice. He is able to deal with it. Many cruel things were done and said about Jesus and yet He did not take justice into His own hands.

I Peter 2:23 – He did not retaliate when He was insulted, nor threaten revenge when He suffered. He left his case in the hands of God, who always judges fairly.

EARL'S STORY:

Earl was very angry at his mom. She had done something to him when he was five-years old, something that he felt was exceptionally unjust. He hated her. For over two decades, he carried this anger. He kept his anger because he was not going to let his mom get away with it. She deserved to have his anger. I asked Earl if his mom knew that he was angry with her and he said that they do not have a relationship. She did not know that he was angry at her. Earl's anger was poisoning him; he was the one being punished.

When he realized how very futile his anger was, he made the choice to give his anger to God. He also placed his mom in God's hands, so He could deal with her. After the prayer and the giving of his anger to God, I asked God if He had anything to say to this young man. All of a sudden, Earl blurted out that his mom had not realized what she was doing to him as a child. She did not have a good mother growing up and so did not know how to be a good mom to him. Forgiveness flowed from Earl's heart to his mom. He cried out, "I love my mom. I want my mom!"

That is what the release of anger looks like. Anger was gone when there was no reason to keep it. A huge transformation happened before my eyes. He was set free, free from carrying the huge burden of anger towards his mom.

Anger may be directed towards one's self, keeping ourselves accountable, instead of accusing others. Anger can be a slave-driver, continuously tormenting your mind. Jesus was beaten so we could be whole, He was whipped so we could be healed.[110] He has already dealt with your shortcomings, your sin. He knows all about it and He has taken your punishment. There is no need to keep anger to punish yourself. Give it to Jesus, then set yourself free by forgiving yourself. Free and full of joy.

KERRY'S STORY:

Kerry was angry with herself for making bad choices. She needed anger to hold herself accountable for what she had done, so that she would never do it again. It was difficult for Kerry to verbalize what had happened to her.

Her event took place one evening while in Grade ten, when she snuck out of the house to party. She ended up drunk. When under the influence of alcohol, she was raped by two guys. She felt incredibly guilty for placing herself in this

---

[110] Isaiah 53:5

situation. She had made a mistake and lost her virginity. Her future was destroyed.

Jesus knows what happened. He died so that Kerry does not have to live with the guilt and shame. Kerry gave Jesus her anger and received forgiveness from Him. She extended forgiveness to those two young men who sinned against her. She also forgave herself, for she did not realize what would happen as a result of sneaking out to go to the drinking party. Her anger was no longer needed, she was free to live. Jesus will stay by her side. He adores her.

Sometimes, anger is kept as motivation to never do that horrid thing again. If you want anger to motivate you, it will eventually crush your spirit. But if you replace anger with Jesus, He will breathe life into your being. He will guide and direct you through His Spirit.[111] Give your anger to Him.

3. Anger gives us a sense of control and power.

In reality, the injustice of the situation makes you feel out of control, weak and vulnerable. Anger makes you feel dominant and powerful. Anger builds a wall to protect yourself from more pain. People withdraw. It prevents meaningful relationships and keeps God out. Anger isolates you, making you angrier. Anger causes you to be out of control and alone. That is not living; that is dying.

Parents may use anger towards their children in order to motivate and control them. Anger makes the parent feel powerful, instead of feeling the fear of inadequacy and no control. God asks fathers not to provoke their child to anger by the way they treat them.[112] The power of anger may have been modeled by their parents, demonstrating anger to be a way of dealing with pain.

---

[111] John 16:13
[112] Ephesians 6:4

117

PRAYER: Giving anger to God

Lord, I am so angry at (name of person) for (what they did). I have held onto this anger because (which of the three reasons), but it's not working. Anger is destroying me. I don't want this anger anymore. I give it to you. It is all yours. You are a just God so I choose to trust you with this person. I put this person in your hands so you can deal with them in your justice, knowing that you are also a compassionate God. Lord, I ask you to bless this person because they really did not know what they were doing. I choose to forgive them for the same reason that you forgive me. Thank you for your love. Fill me with your peace. Thank you, Lord!

PRAYER: Regarding long-standing anger

Lord, when I was a child in the memory of (recall the time), I allowed anger into my life. I have allowed it to be part of my life in order to cope with my pain. I didn't know that I could do something with it other than harbour it. I have allowed anger to be my bodyguard. I tell this anger to leave my life in the name of Jesus. I don't want it to be living in my house anymore. Anger is 'fired' as my bodyguard and in its place, I ask you, Jesus, to be my bodyguard. You understand me and only You can heal my pain. Come with me into my pain and heal me. I open my heart wide to you, fill me with your love. Fill me with your Spirit. I receive your peace and your joy!

ANGRY AT GOD:

What if you are angry at God? Sometimes it feels like you have a good reason to be angry at Him. Maybe you have no one else to blame, and dare not blame yourself, so hold God responsible.

Proverbs 19:3 - People ruin their lives by their own foolishness and then are angry at the Lord.

Perhaps God disappointed you in some way or let you down. He did not fulfil your expectations. Bring your grievance to Him and be willing to hear His words.

Several years ago, I awoke one morning with my mind fuming – at God. I had been praying and fasting, doing my part, but He was doing – nothing. I told God my grievances, then was quiet to listen to Him. I will never forget what He spoke into my mind. He said that He was the One who makes the sun rise every morning, not too early and not too late. It will come up at just the right time. Just so, when it is time to answer my prayer, it will happen, not too early and not too late. He hears my prayers and will answer them at just the right time. My response was: "Oh Lord! If it's not the right time, please don't answer this prayer right now. I will trust you. And thank you Lord."

In order to hear God's words, you must be willing to hear Him. Put down your hand of 'not' listening to Him, and look into His face - then listen.

PRAYER: regarding Anger towards God
Dear God, I am angry at You for (reason why). This gives me a lot of pain. Anger is destroying me and I'm a mess. I am ready to hear from You. I put down my anger and choose to listen to You. Please speak to me.

Ask Him if He has anything to say to you. Listen to His voice. His words will not only set you free, but they will breathe life into the core of your being.

When we agree to give our anger to God, He will fill us with His peace. When we give our anger to God, we are agreeing that it is no longer up to us to try to make it fair. We trust in God; He is a just God. He will take care of it.

Yet the Lord longs to be gracious to you;
therefore, He will rise up
to show you compassion.
For the Lord is a God of justice.
Blessed are all who wait for Him!
– Isaiah 30:18 (NIV)

REFLECTIONS: Chapter 8 – The Wall of Anger

1. Why would someone build a wall of anger?
2. How did God deal with Cain's anger?
   What was his warning?
3. Anger is about an injustice. Who are you angry at? Why?
4. It is okay to be angry, but not okay to keep it.
   Why would you keep anger?
5. What can you do with anger towards others?
   Towards God?
6. Why is trusting God such an important part of giving Him
   your anger?

Notes & Journaling:

PART 4

Experiencing Jesus

Just knowing about Jesus is not
enough, He must be
experienced.

He adores us.
We were created
as His masterpiece.
Unique and amazing.

Jesus has always been with us,
is with us now, and always will be.

Jesus understands pain,
He has experienced it all.
He is our Healer.

Chapter 9

In the Womb

I read an article in the New York Post, July 11, 2017, regarding an incredible pregnancy. It was not just an ordinary pregnancy. It was extraordinary.

Most pregnancies produce one baby. This unique pregnancy involved two babies. But that is not what makes it extraordinary. There have been many twins throughout the world.

Normal generally means that the pregnancy takes nine months, give, or take a week or two. This pregnancy took seven months. Birth at seven months gestation is not uncommon, though not normal. Premature babies can and do thrive, and medical advances make that possible.

Normal is the mother being in her 20s to 30s. The mother of these particular twins was not as young as the Peruvian mother, age five years, seven months, and 17 days[113]; nor was she too old like, 70-year-old, Rajo Devi Iohan of India.[114] This mom was age twenty-one. A common age. Yet this pregnancy was exceptional.

Normal is the mother giving nourishment to the developing fetus. This mother, Frankielen da Silva Zampoli Padilha was 9 weeks pregnant when she had a massive stroke.[115] She was brain dead for most of her pregnancy. With the help of life support for the mom, the hearts of the twins, kept beating. The

---

[113] Stephanie Dawson (editor), Oldest and Youngest Mothers by PositiveMed-team, n.d., Positivemed.com.
[114] Ibid.
[115] Tamar Lapin, Brain-dead woman kept alive for months so she could deliver twins, New York Post, July 11, 2017, mypost.com

doctors did all they could to support the underdeveloped lives within the womb. Day by day, 123 days to be exact,[116] these two babies were nurtured within the body of their brain-dead mother. Countless specialists committed themselves to keeping them alive.

Studies have proven that a baby is affected by what is happening outside the womb.[117] Music was played for the babies. Doctors and caregivers sang regularly to them.[118] At 7 months gestation, the twins were born. Except for being premature, these babies had developed perfectly. Dr. Rivabem said that the care and commitment of the medical staff and 'divine purpose' made this miracle possible.[119] In the darkness and warmth of the womb, God was present. What an amazing story. What an amazing Creator we have.

Psalm 139:13,15 - You made all the delicate, inner parts of my body and knit me together in my mother's womb. You watched me as I was being formed in utter seclusion, as I was woven together in the dark of the womb.

God is the 'knitter' of our formation within the womb. If someone does not know how to knit, the yarn is just string and the knitting needles are just pointy sticks. But a creative knitter can intricately maneuver the yarn, using knitting needles, creating an interlocking pattern. One long piece of string becomes a superb garment. Knitting produces an amazing creation at the hands of a skilled knitter. It is the knitter who takes credit, not the wool nor the needles.

God uses the tissue that He created, to form the different parts of the human body. Tenderly He designs various delicate systems and intricate functioning of this

---

[116] Tamar Lapin, Brain-dead woman kept alive for months so she could deliver twins, New York Post, July 11, 2017, mypost.com

[117] Noelia de la Cruz, Your Baby's Journey from Conception to Birth, Parents, n.d., parents.com

[118] Tamar Lapin, Brain-dead woman kept alive for months so she could deliver twins, New York Post, July 11, 2017, mypost.com

[119] Tanveer Mann, Brain dead mother gives birth to twins after 123 days on life support, July 11, 2017, metro.co.uk

amazing formation, placing all the parts exactly where they need to be. It reflects the creativity of the One who does the knitting. That is our God. He has knit us together in our mothers' womb. He is the One who determines the pattern to create, making each of us unique and perfect for His purpose.

My eldest daughter has brown eyes while her husband's eyes are hazel. Yet their oldest and youngest sons have bright blue eyes. My youngest daughter has chocolate brown eyes and her husband has hazel eyes yet their daughter has the most beautiful blue eyes possible. God delights in being creative.

He determines the one unique male sperm to penetrate the waiting one-of-a-kind female egg. An embryo forms which evolves into a magnificent, unique baby. God is the Master designer and the One who has purpose in creating us exactly how we are. He is the One who determines our personality and character, gifts, and abilities. He is with us in the darkness of the womb, and He thinks about us all the time.[120] He tenderly loves us, determining every day that we are to live. God has been with us right from the moment of conception.

GOD DETERMINES CONCEPTION:
God is the One who governs conception. He opens and closes the womb.

- Abraham and Sarah were promised descendants that would outnumber the stars. The promised conception happened when Sarah was thought to be too old to have children[121] and Abraham was 100 years old.[122] God said that the birth of baby Isaac was at just the right time. [123]
- Jacob married two wives. He was tricked into marrying the oldest daughter, Leah, but it was the younger

---

[120] Psalm 139:17-18
[121] Hebrews 11:11
[122] Genesis 21:5
[123] Genesis 21:2

daughter, Rachel, whom he loved. God had compassion on Leah and gave her four sons. Rachel had none; her womb was closed. Rachel was angry at Jacob for not giving her sons. Jacob exclaimed that it was God who was keeping her from having children.[124] Later, in the midst of Rachel's crying out to God, He enabled her to have a son.[125] God was in charge.

God created you and me; we are His masterpiece. Nobody and nothing can negate our worth. A damaged $100 bill is still worth $100 no matter what its condition. It has value because its worth is determined by its creator. Just so, our worth is stamped upon each of us because of our Creator. He is our Artist, the One who designed us. We are perfect to Him, bringing delight to the Creator.

Psalm 139:14 - Thank you for making me so wonderfully complex! Your workmanship is marvellous – how well I know it.

When I was pregnant with my second child, Cherie, God tenderly knit her together. She was not formed perfectly, according to our world's standards, being blind and having cerebral palsy. Doctors thought I had come in contact with a virus, during the first or second-month of my pregnancy, causing damage to her developing eyes and cerebral tissue.

When Cherie was approximately 30 years of age, I interviewed her in a class that I taught. It was obvious that her eyes were abnormal, causing blindness, and the walker displayed her inability to walk independently. Her difficulties were visible and she was thrilled to share with others how she dealt with her challenges. At the beginning of my class, I asked her to tell everyone what was wrong with her. She was not

---

[124] Genesis 30:2
[125] Genesis 20:32

taken aback by my request, and stated, "There's nothing wrong with me." She was firm in speaking those words, for she believed them with her whole heart. And it was true. God did not make a mistake. There was nothing wrong with her. She was exactly who she was meant to be. She was magnificent. She had an unusual story to tell and her inspiration touched many.

To be created in His image means we are similar to God. God is Spirit,[126] so the likeness is not about the physical make up but about the core of our being. Socially, we are created for relationships just like our God who is communal, three in one – Father, Son and Holy Spirit. We share His emotions – joy, sadness, patience, anger, delight, jealousy, etc. He feels and touches; He hears and speaks; He sees, tastes and smells. The Spirit of God fits perfectly within our spirit.

When I began exploring inner healing within the womb, it felt odd. But I sensed God's Spirit guide me to continue following His lead. Research reveals that babies can feel what is going on while in the womb. Studies conclude that the baby begins to hear in the second trimester of formation. They begin to recognize voices.[127]

The physician-author of the book of Luke, wrote that Mary, when she was told she would be Jesus' mother, visited her relative Elizabeth who was six months pregnant at that time. Luke goes on to say that when Mary greeted Elizabeth, the baby within Elizabeth leapt for joy.[128] The baby sensed that he was in the presence of the Son of God.

JILL'S STORY:

Jill's gait was affected because of cerebral palsy. She was angry at God for the hardships and limitations she

---

[126] John 4:24
[127] Noelia de la Cruz, Pregnancy and Birth; Your Baby's Journey from Conception to Birth, n.d., Parents.com
[128] Luke 1:41

experienced. This caused her to feel undesirable, and she had a fear that no man would ever like her. Jill thought she was not pretty and had no worth. This young lady remembered looking at a photo album of her baby pictures, thinking she looked disgusting, with dark eyes.

I asked her to imagine herself in the womb where God was knitting her together. When she was there, she sensed the joy that God had as He was creating her. He was smiling and whispering into her ear, telling her that she was beautiful.

A transformation occurred. When Jill recalled the album of baby photos, the baby's eyes were radiant, reflecting light instead of darkness. Jill remembered the next photo, where she was in the incubator and she felt happiness for the baby. As she flicked through the photos in her mind, she heard Jesus' words that she was beautiful, stunning. Jill's soul filled with delight and joy.

Isaiah 49:1 – The Lord called me before my birth, from within the womb He called me by name.

GEORGINA'S STORY:
When Georgina imagined herself in the womb, she sensed a swirling blackness of negativity, an angry darkness. It was incredibly heavy, extremely lethal. Jesus was not to be found anywhere – but He spoke to her and said that He was there, even in the darkness of the womb.[129]

I asked Jesus if He had anything to say to the tiny little baby girl. His words were tender and soothing, they spoke of comfort and peace - He loved her deeply and will always be with her. The little baby's heart became relieved. She saw a faint brightness in the distance – "Invite the light to come closer, baby girl".

---

[129] Psalm 139:12

As Jesus came, she felt warmth and happiness invade her soul. He was there; He had always been there for her. The little girl gave the hatred and anger to Jesus. It was her mom who was angry. Her mom brought shame upon the family, by being pregnant with this baby. Jesus told Georgina that she was loved very much. This little baby girl felt a freedom from the darkness. Peace came upon her. She saw a picture in her mind of a shimmering crown on her head and a little sparkling cape adorning her body. She was prancing around, singing and dancing. Georgina's heart was full of joy. She was loved and accepted.

Psalm 139:17-18 - How precious are your thoughts about me, O God. They cannot be numbered! I can't even count them; they outnumber the grains of sand! And when I wake up, you are still with me!

LORRIE ANN'S STORY:

Lorrie Ann met with me for Inner Healing and said that she sensed there was something that kept her from living fully for God. She was aware of a darkness. I invited her to go into the womb. When there, she sensed a thick darkness and could not see Jesus. He showed her that it was the presence of death, darkness, and suicide. Her father had raped her mother, and Lorrie Ann was the result of that violent act. As Lorrie Ann invited the light, it grew and came closer. I asked her if she could see the hand of this little developing baby.

"Yes", she replied.

"Can you see Jesus' hand?"

Again, her answer was, "Yes".

I encouraged her to hold His hand. Jesus cuddled her and spoke of His great love for her. Lorrie Ann did not want this darkness to stay so she told it to leave in the name of Jesus.

Everything became peaceful and surreal. The darkness was gone.

Psalm 139:12 – Even in the darkness I cannot hide from you. To you the night shines as bright as day. Darkness and light are the same for you.

ROBERT'S STORY:

Robert felt trapped within the womb, felt that he needed to get out of there because he was getting hurt. He was not wanted. The little developing baby curled tighter in his fetal position, afraid of what was happening on the outside. He had to escape. He sensed Jesus laying down beside him, protecting him. Peace filled his little being. He was blessed to be given life.

Today, God is using this man to bring encouragement and speak the good news of Jesus into many people's lives. He has distributed countless Bibles into the hands of those who needed hope. The resurrecting power of Jesus infiltrated his heart.

Jeremiah 1:5 – I knew you before I formed you in your mother's womb. Before you were born, I set you apart and appointed you as my prophet to the nations.

INGRID'S STORY:

A middle-aged woman, Ingrid, had indents on her skull, like scars, and now she knows why. She was recently told that her parents had tried to abort her. Forceps had tried to end her life. She was angry and furious at her parents because they did not want her.

Her mother had a nervous breakdown before Ingrid was born. Since Ingrid was the last baby of a long string of children in her family, she felt nobody had time for her. This woman felt sad that she was alive.

When imagining herself in the womb, Ingrid felt uncomfortable, as though she did not belong. Jesus was present; He was protecting her little body. He spoke to this forming baby and said that she was His, He was the One creating her. She had been created so she could take care of other children; the downcast, abandoned and rejected. Jesus told her that scars can heal. He understood pain. Jesus too had scars that portrayed how much He loved her. They are evidence that He died for her.

Jesus went on to say that her parents were too overwhelmed to have another child. Ingrid needed to forgive them because they did not know what they were doing when trying to abort her.

"Little girl, let go of all the pain, bitterness and anger. Lean on Him and not on your own understanding."

Ingrid gave Him her pain. He removed it. She was safe, loved, valued, treasured, and had a purpose, a reason to be alive.

But Ingrid's anger flared up again. She left my office angry. Several months later she attended an Inner Healing Seminar and gave God all her anger. She was now free to live, to have joy. That is what Jesus does. Liberates the captive. Sets us free to live – abundantly.

Psalm 139:16 – You saw me before I was born. Every day of my life was recorded in your book. Every moment was laid out before a single day had passed.

ABORTION:

There is inner healing for those who are guilty of aborting their baby. Maybe it was your choice to abort the foetus. Maybe you were coerced or did not know of any other solution. Jesus did not come to condemn you, but to save you.[130] He

---

[130] John 3:17

understands. He died for your guilt – to set you free, to have peace, to live without the heaviness of guilt. Give it to Him. He is waiting for you to receive His gift of forgiveness. He absolutely adores you.

PRAYER: Forgiveness for Abortion
Dear Lord Jesus. I'm so sorry for ending the life of my little baby. I didn't know what else to do; I didn't know what I was doing. I feel so guilty for my actions. I'm so sorry. Please forgive me. I give you all my guilt. I don't want it anymore. Cleanse my heart and set me free of this huge weight. Thank you for dying for my guilt, my sin. Thank you that I don't have to carry this heavy burden of guilt and shame. Thank you for taking it. It comforts me to know you have my little baby and one day I will see him/her. Until that day, fill me with your peace and hold me, dear Jesus. Pour your love into my heart. I give it to you. Thank you that You know everything about me and You love me dearly. Thank you that You do have a good plan for my life. I give you my life, I choose to follow You. Hold me tight as I look into your eyes. You are a magnificent Father. Breathe your life into my being. In the name of Jesus, Amen.

God delights in you. He adores you no matter what you have done or have not done. His love is unconditional. He created you specifically for a reason. He has put within you exactly what you need, in order to fulfil His purpose. He is the One who knit you together in your mother's womb. He held you from the moment of conception and keeps holding you. Every day – He was present, is present, and will always be present. You are magnificently created. It is true.

For the Spirit of God has made me,

and the breath of the Almighty

gives me life.

- Job 33:8

REFLECTIONS: Chapter 9 – Even in the Womb

PSALMS 139: 1-18

Verses 1-4 - O Lord, you have examined my heart and know everything about me. You know when I sit down or stand up. You know my thoughts even when I'm far away. You see me when I travel and when I rest at home. You know everything I do. You know what I am going to say even before I say it, Lord.

1. How does it feel, believing that God knows EVERYTHING about you and loves you deeply?

_____

_____

_____

_____

_____

_____

_____

_____

_____

_____

_____

_____

Verses 5-6 - You go before me and follow me. You place your hand of blessing on my head. Such knowledge is too wonderful for me, too great for me to understand!

2. How does it make you feel that God is placing His hand of blessing upon you? What kind of blessing do you long for?

_____

_____

_____

_____

_____

_____

_____

_____

_____

_____

Verses 7-12 - I can never escape from your Spirit! I can never get away from your presence! If I go up to heaven, you are there; if I go down to the grave, you are there. If I ride the wings of the morning, if I dwell by the farthest oceans, even there your hand will guide me, and your strength will support me. I could ask the darkness to hide me and the light around me to become night but even in darkness I cannot hide from you. For you, the night shines as bright as day. Darkness and light are the same to you.

3. How does it feel that Jesus is with you? Always has been with you. Always will be.

_____

_____

_____

_____

_____

Verses 13-16 - You made all the delicate, inner parts of my body and knit me together in my mother's womb. Thank you for making me so wonderfully complex! Your workmanship is marvellous- how well I know it. You watched me as I was being formed in utter seclusion, as I was woven together in the dark of the womb. You saw me before I was born. Every day of my life was recorded in your book. Every moment was laid out before a single day had passed.

4. God made you unique. What is special about you?

_____

_____

_____

_____

_____

_____

_____

_____

_____

_____

_____

_____

_____

Verses 17-18 - How precious are your thoughts about me, O God. They cannot be numbered! I can't even count them; they outnumber the grains of sand! When I wake up, you are still with me!

5. You are precious to Him. Receive His love into your heart. Let Him totally fill it. How does it make you feel?

_____

_____

_____

_____

_____

_____

Chapter 10

Jesus in Pain

Pain seizes one's emotions. It is heavy and overwhelming. Lonely. It feels violent and ruthless, penetrating the depths of one's soul.

JESUS IN HIS PAIN:
God the Father planned for His Son to endure a violent death. Jesus endured pain to its depth – physically, mentally, emotionally, and spiritually. He underwent every type of pain possible, all alone. End of life by crucifixion was cruel, humiliating, and public.

Death on the cross was unbearable pain.[131] The condemned person had nails driven through his wrists and feet, anchoring him to the cross beams. All the weight of the body hung from his shoulders. It was exhausting and the pain screamed from within – but it was unheard, muted – for his chest cavity could not contract to expel air from his lungs – unless the man shifted his weight onto his nailed feet. It was torturous pain that seemed unending.

Succumbing to death, by crucifixion, could take days, depending on the environment, the condition of the body, and the method used. Sometimes the soldiers shattered the leg bones to quicken death. The lungs could not exhale, the carbon dioxide mounted, the blood was not able to circulate and the organs began to fail. Shock set in. This was the death that Father God planned for His Son to endure. When the

---

[131] Wikipedia, Last edited by Rathfelder, Crucifixion, en.m.wikipedia.org

soldiers came to check on Jesus, he had already expired. But to confirm his death, they pierced his side with a spear. A mixture of blood and water flowed out from His chest cavity.

I have watched the movie: The Passion. It tears my heart to see the cruelty done to the Son of God. He was mocked, spit on, accused, jeered at, betrayed, and abandoned – then a thorny crown was pressed onto His head. His beard hairs were yanked out of their pores. His face violently slapped and His body mercilessly lashed with a lead-tipped whip that ripped chunks of flesh from His body. He was unrecognizable after the torturous thrashing. Then He was nailed to a cross.

Throughout the Old Testament, the happenings of Jesus' death were predicted and fulfilled.

ISAIAH PROPHESIED:
- Jesus was scourged and mocked while He suffered[132]
- He would not defend Himself.[133]

ZECHARIAH SAID:
- Jesus' body would be pierced.[134]

PSALMS STATES:
- Jesus' body would be mutilated[135]
- His hands and feet would be pierced[136]
- He would be given vinegar to drink[137]
- Not one of His bones would be broken[138]

---

[132] Isaiah 50:6 & Matthew 27:26-30
[133] Isaiah 53:7 & Matthew 27:13-14
[134] Zechariah 12:10 & John 19:34, 37
[135] Psalm 22:16 & John 19:1
[136] Psalm 22:16 & Mark 15:25
[137] Psalm 69:21 & Matthew 27:34
[138] Psalm 34:20 & John 19:32-33, 36

- His garments would be divided[139]
- Jesus would die as a condemned criminal[140]
- His words spoken on the cross were prophesized[141]

This agonizing death was planned by Father God. It was no mistake; it was His intention, even before the world was in existence.[142]

Isaiah 53:10 – It was the Lord's good plan to crush Him and cause Him grief.

I think of the many surgeries that my daughter underwent throughout her years. I was the one who signed the papers, knowing that she would have intense agony. I was the one to cause the procedure of unbearable pain. I loved her, more than words could describe, and that was why I gave permission for the surgeon to proceed. If there had been an easier way of achieving what needed to be done, I certainly would have done that – but there was no easier way that I knew of. I believed it was worth going through the tremendous physical and emotional suffering because I believed that better things would come as a result. It saved her life.

Jesus' mission was to die for our guilt. This assignment could have been accomplished much easier, had the soldiers beheaded Him. Beheading a person was common in those days. They could have killed Him and His blood would have covered our guilt; our debt would have been paid in full; a quick and easy death. But instead, Jesus' death was horrendous, taking place before thousands of eyes.

Father God did not choose the easy route. This way of suffering was the hardest possible, but there was a reason. By

---

[139] Psalm 22:18 & John 19:24
[140] Psalm 69:19-20 & Matthew 27:46
[141] Psalm 22:1 & Matthew 27:46
[142] Ephesians 1:4-7

going down this Via Delarosa, the Way of Suffering, He identified with every deep emotion that we could possibly experience. He was:

- betrayed by one of his chosen disciples[143]
- abandoned and deserted by his friends[144]
- spat in the face and beaten by the spiritual leaders[145]
- falsely accused, lied about[146]
- denied by his closest friends, of knowing Him[147]
- rejected, ridiculed, and humiliated[148]
- scourged with a lead-tipped whip[149]
- mocked and dressed up to be a king[150]
- called a liar, scoffed, and sneered at – He could not even save Himself[151]
- alone, felt abandoned by His Father[152]

Isaiah 53:5 – He was pierced for our rebellion, crushed for our sins. He was beaten so we could be whole. He was whipped so we could be healed.

JESUS IN MY PAIN:

The world is full of anguish; pain exists in all of our societies. It pierces everyone; no one is untouchable.

- My daughter-in-law just had a baby. Labour was strenuous work and painful.
- A family member was put into a semi-coma because his cancerous pain was too much to bear.

---

[143] Matthew 26:14-16, Mark 14:44-45
[144] Matthew 26:56
[145] Matthew 26:67
[146] Matthew 26:59
[147] Matthew 26:74
[148] Mark 15:29-30
[149] Matthew 27:26
[150] Mark 15:17-20
[151] Matthew 27:41-44
[152] Mark 15:34

- A long-drawn-out divorce was endured, the heart betrayed, shattered into fragments.
- A boss ridiculed his employee, calling him a loser, a failure with no future.
- A parent took out their anger on an innocent child, suffocating any hope of love.
- My daughter died and my soul gasped to breathe.

Jesus understands pain, knows what it feels like. It happened to Him while on Earth, and now He stands beside us when we suffer. His presence surrounds us. He has not forgotten us; He knows our names.[153] He loves us with an everlasting love – forever. With unfailing love, He draws us to Him.[154]

Jesus chose to give up His rights as God and obey His Father in His suffering. He became totally vulnerable and gave up His godly power in order to fulfil His Father's plan. He could have called thousands of angels to protect Him, but He did not.[155] Jesus experienced the shredding of the soul, scourging of his body, torturing of His mind, feeling that His Father had abandoned Him. He knows what it feels like because He experienced it. He is the only One who truly understands our soul in our darkest hours, days, weeks, even years. Jesus knows what piercing pain feels like and He is right beside us. He has not forsaken us nor does He look the other way. He is very present; His heart knows all about pain. He understands.

ABIGAIL:

Abigail, just six years old, was angry at God. She felt betrayed and let down. Her wounded heart oozed with deep agony. She said that Jesus was cruel for He did not answer her prayers. She wanted her mom and dad to love each other. Her heart cried out to Jesus – then she gave up. Her mom and dad still

---

[153] Isaiah 49:15-16
[154] Jeremiah 31:3
[155] Matthew 26:53-54

yelled at each other. Little Abigail believed that Jesus was not answering her heart-felt cry; He did not care. She felt worthless, of no value. Abigail confided in me that she was a bad girl. Her sorrowful eyes looked at me with self-loathing condemnation. The wounds of her soul lingered – haunting her, condemning her, suffocating all hope.

Life moves on and circumstances change but Abigail's belief will remain very much alive – unless Jesus speaks to her. Jesus understands her pain. He too was at the mercy of other people's choices.

Childhood experiences establish beliefs within the mind of the child. Children are not able to understand the big picture of why someone would hurt them. Painful words and actions bring woundedness; absence of tender words and actions also bring wounds to the soul. A child only knows how it makes them feel.

Pain becomes a reoccurring theme in life, generating beliefs that they are:
- Worthless
- Ugly
- Alone
- Unloved
- Filled with fault
- Flawed
- Unprotected and vulnerable
- Invisible
- Hopeless
- Helpless
- Powerless

God created us with coping mechanisms in order to survive. The child may escape what is happening by going somewhere else, in their mind, while it is occurring. At times, they numb themselves to the pain, remembering what happened but not feeling the emotions. Sometimes anger takes over, to protect them from being crushed by the pain. Or their mind goes into denial and chooses to forget what happened, suppressing their memory. Another personality may develop, in order to compartmentalize that part of their life. The child may develop excessive compulsive habits in order to feel like they have some order and control. Whatever their way of dealing with the pain, its purpose is to cope with it and try to keep living. It is a survival mechanism.

As the child grows into a teenager, then an adult, he/she gains power and the consequences of the belief magnifies. There are more options in dealing with the pain, to numb it or to fill the immense void in their souls.
There are all sorts of ways to cope:
- Drinking
- Drugs
- Sex
- Pornography
- Food
- Gangs
- Anger
- Shopping
- Movies
- Gaming
- Staying busy
- Excessive exercise.

In the center of all these coping mechanisms, there is the vacuum of not being loved, of not being accepted, nor belonging to anyone. These painful beliefs need to be transformed, resulting in different behaviour. The truth of Jesus is urgently needed.

ILLUSTRATION:

We looked out the window and saw billowing black smoke coming from behind the building. After investigation, we discovered a car engulfed in flames. The pitch-black smoke generated gigantic puffs. The fire department was alerted, and when they arrived, the firemen positioned massive fans to blow the smoke away. This is ridiculous. Absurd.

Though smoke could be controlled by funneling it, capturing it, or even capping it, this solution was temporary for the smoke kept coming. It took a lot of energy to control it, and eventually we gave up trying to contain it. Controlling the smoke was not the solution; extinguishing the fire would eliminate the smoke.

Similarly, we tend to focus on the behaviour instead of understanding what has caused the behaviour, where the pain is coming from. Follow the trail of emotion and it will reveal where the belief was formed. A childhood memory is where the 'fire', the painful belief, began. This belief feels so very true and the behaviour billows out from it.

Jesus was with you when the painful belief was ignited within your soul. He knows what is true about you, and it is His words that transform painful lies to peaceful truth. When this transformation happens, new behaviour will flow. When truth is received from Jesus, there is freedom to thrive.

We must allow the doctor to see the wound, before he can bring healing to it. Just so, the pain must be exposed in order to receive healing from Jesus. He is gentle and compassionate. He understands:

- Betrayal
- Abuse
- Abandonment
- Rejection
- Wrongful accusations
- Mocking and humiliation

- Vulnerability

The Healer is right beside you. Jesus understands your wounds. He alone can extinguish the lies that feel so very true, that are so painful. He was present when it happened to you. Come to Him. He is your Healer.

VALERIE'S STORY:

Valerie followed her painful emotions back to a memory. She burst out crying, exclaiming that she could not go back to that incident.

"No, please no!" It caused excruciating pain. Her soul was torn apart, so vulnerable. It was too difficult to think about it; her emotions were out of control.

I asked her to go to a memory where she sensed the presence of Jesus. She went into that memory and her heart basked in His presence, then she brought Jesus with her into her heart-wrenching memory. Now, with Jesus at her side, she felt:

- Safety
- Connected
- Warmth
- Loved, cherished
- Hopeful

Jesus spoke truth into her painful belief and she received it. Healing took place. Peace for her soul.

In our lives, His Presence can be sensed:

- at a specific location – in a church, at an important function or possibly in a jail cell.
- with a person who loves, prays, gives into our need, hugs us.
- at a celebration – a milestone in life, a wedding/birth
- during a crisis – when we hurt, could have died in the midst of a dreaded disease, the death of a loved one.

- in His magnificent nature – a serene lakeside, sunrise, or beautiful landscape.

There was a 'knowing' in this memory that Jesus was beside us, that He was present. Jesus is our Healer. Allow Him into our pain. He is gentle and loves us deeply.

SHANNON'S STORY:

Shannon relived her painful memory; Jesus was sensed to be present. A three-way conversation took place between Shannon, Jesus, and me. I, as facilitator, asked Jesus questions. He answered with thoughts into her mind. Shannon shared them with me. This triune communication flowed smoothly, like a well-greased machine, prompting me to ask Jesus another question. In the midst of her painful memory, Jesus invited her to come to Him and she gave her life to Him. Then we invited Jesus' words of healing into her painful memory. Peace filled her soul; joy spilled from her heart. Today, Shannon is immensely grateful for knowing that Jesus is always with her. It is true, she is loved by Him.

During an Inner Healing Session, when individuals went back into a painful childhood memory, some:

- **SAW JESUS BESIDE THEM.**
They turned and faced Him, looked into His eyes, inviting Jesus into their pain. Love started to flow from His eyes to the child's, filled up their heart. He spoke truth and the truth set them free.
  - A young boy was thrown down the stairs by his partying parents. The door was slammed shut. He felt rejected and alone. Heartbroken. He looked around in the memory and saw Jesus playing trucks with him. He realized he was not alone. Jesus' presence brought him

comfort and value. Jesus wanted to be with him. The grown man now chuckled in delight, for he realized that every time his parents disposed of him into the basement, he was able to spend time with Jesus, playing with his toys.

- Thomas was at the beach by himself, lonely and rejected. Jesus was holding out His hand. He was not alone; Jesus was always with him. They walked hand in hand along the path through the woods.

- Anita was sexually molested. She saw Jesus crying for her, beside her bed. His deep compassion flowed over her and over the offender. Jesus spoke into her mind, filling her with comfort and peace. "It's not your fault", "You are okay", "I love you", "You are beautiful".

- Geraldine had terrifying memories of her stepdad beating her mercilessly. Nobody believed that it was happening. Geraldine felt there was something wrong with her. Her soul was filled with hopelessness, there was no one to protect her. She closed her eyes and looked around in the memory. Jesus was right beside her, holding her hand. He told her that she was beautiful and deeply cherished. Jesus filled her heart with overwhelming joy as she forgave her stepdad. Fear left her, for Jesus was always with her. Her heart felt like there were fireworks going off, celebrating who she was.

- **SAW JESUS STANDING AT A DISTANCE** – outside the door or nearby.
  - Jane painfully remembered waiting for dreaded news at the doctor's office. When asked where Jesus was, she said that He was in the waiting room. He was a gentleman, waiting for her to invite Him in with her. She invited Him into the room where she was. The fear left her, and instead, her heart was at peace.

149

- **SENSED JESUS.**
  - One little girl saw a street light shining through her window, and sensed that it was Jesus looking down upon her. She asked Jesus to be in the room with her. He came close beside her. Peace flowed upon her.

- **SENSED JESUS IN A PERSON** - like a grandmother or a neighbour.
  - Kaetlyn's house was on fire in the middle of the night. She sensed Jesus waking her up. The flames and smoke were terrifying. A tall man whom she assumed to be her neighbour, rushed into the house to help her sleeping family escape the consuming flames. It was Jesus working through a person. Her whole family was safe. Jesus was with them. Instead of terror, there was amazement of God's presence and His peace.

The presence of Jesus negates the belief that we are alone. His presence drives away fear; His words transform pain into peace. The painful memory becomes a place of a sweet, sacred remembrance of basking in the love of Jesus.

DEALING WITH SHAME:

Shame may be put on a child by speaking degrading and condemning words or actions. Shame is a thick, heavy, grotesque coat which suffocates life. Jesus understands shame for it was heaped upon Him as He hung on the cross.

Jesus has taken all our shame. We do not have to carry it anymore. He forgave those who ridiculed and mocked Him. Forgiveness breaks the cycle of shame; unforgiveness keeps the pain alive, allowing shame to overshadow us. We can give our shame to Jesus; we do not have to carry it anymore.

Isaiah 53:3 – He was despised and rejected - a man of sorrows, acquainted with deepest grief. We turned our backs on Him and looked the other way. He was despised, and we did not care.

TINA'S STORY:

Tina felt worthless because she was a girl and not a boy. To her, being a girl meant that she was of a lower class than males, becoming their servant with no rights of her own. She carried a deep heaviness of shame. Jesus spoke to her, telling her that He died for her shame. Tina gave Him her coat of shame and in its place, clothed her in ivory silk pajamas. She was thrilled. Her heart felt light and clean.

Jesus put her heart's shattered pieces together. It became a work of beauty, just like the Japanese art called Kintsugi, where broken pottery pieces are mended with lacquer, mixed with gold, silver, or platinum. She was exactly as God made her to be and she was safe. Jesus will always be there for her because she has a special place in His heart.

The presence of Jesus transforms deep wounding memories into a place of sacredness; the memory now holds peace and satisfaction. The incredible presence of Jesus causes transformation and it is a beautiful experience. It is a mystery, an evolvement of something into a new creation, a metamorphosis.

Colossians 3:10 – Put on your new nature and be renewed as you learn to know your Creator and become like Him.

Transformation is an amazing process:
- Jared came for many weekly Inner Healing Sessions. One day he told me that he sensed something was changing inside of him. He could not put his finger on it, but knew he was changing inside. Jesus was present, setting him free.[156] As Jesus spoke into his pain, Jared's soul was

liberated. He was becoming who God had created him to be. Jared's soul soared!

When Jesus speaks into our pain, a new life begins:
- No maintenance is necessary in keeping the inner peace.
- No fighting with the painful beliefs.
- What used to feel like it was true, no longer does.
- Our thoughts and feelings agree. Truth reigns.
- There is no trace of pain in the memory. It has dissipated.
- The memory is remembered but the pain is gone.
- Instead of heaviness and darkness, there is freedom and delight.

It is unexplainable. It is a miracle – one's soul is free.

Isaiah 40:1-3 – I waited patiently for the Lord to help me, and He turned to me and heard my cry. He lifted me out of the pit of despair, out of the mud and the mire. He set my feet on solid ground and steadied me as I walked along. He has given me a new song to sing, a hymn of praise to our God. Many will see what He has done and be amazed. They will put their trust in the Lord.

Jesus invites you to come to Him with your pain, in your darkness. He was there when it happened. He knows pain, and He understands. When you humble yourself and seek Him, He will be found.[157] He was crying with you, holding you, hovering over you, kneeling before you, cradling you in His arms. Give Him your pain and let Him speak His truth into it. He was with you, is with you, and will always be with you – forever.

---

[156] John 8:32
[157] Jeremiah 29:12-14

PRAYER:

Dear Jesus. I have so much pain, have carried it so very long. I am weak, stuck, and tired of this anguish. Give me courage to own it, to feel it, and then invite you into the memory where my painful belief began. I now know that You were in my excruciating pain-filled memory, speak to me what is true. I am open to hear from you. I need your healing. Touch my heart and soul with your love. I come to you. Fill me with your love. Thank you for being my Healer. In Jesus' name, Amen.

The Lord is close to the broken-hearted;

He rescues those whose spirits are crushed.

– Psalm 34:18

1. What kind of pain did Jesus experience during his crucifixion?

2. Jesus understands pain.
   Tell Him about your pain.
   What feels true about yourself? - worthless, helpless, not good enough, powerless, hopeless, alone, unlovable, rejected, abandoned, unwanted, etc.?

3. Go back and 'see' where Jesus is in your painful memory.
   What is He doing?
   "Jesus, is there anything that you want to say to me?"

4. Give Jesus your shame. He has already died for it.
   Forgive your offender.

5. Let Jesus:
   - fill your child-heart with His healing love.
   - hold you in His arms.
   - soothe your soul.
   - speak truth to you.
   - fill you with His love and peace.

Notes & Journaling:

Chapter 11

Their Stories

LILY'S STORY:

As a child, Lily was chided for talking too much. In her memory, Jesus was amused by the feisty words of the seven-year-old girl. He was not offended by her words. Jesus warmed her heart, saying, "I love my chatterbox. Go play in the sunshine."

Little Lily was molested by her dad. She felt dirty, confused and alone. She knew her dad was wrong in what he did to her but she could not tell her mom. She believed it was her fault:

- that her mom left.
- that her dad molested her.
- for her family being evicted from the house.

She saw herself waiting at the bus station, sitting on a bench, feeling like she had lost everything – her family, her house, and all support.

Lily received a picture in her mind, of being adrift on the ocean. Suddenly, Jesus was coming in a boat. He was there to save her but she did not feel that she deserved to be saved. She needed to be punished, not rescued. The little girl had great fear. Lily was dreading the time when her mother would find out. Jesus consoled her. The secret was not hers anymore. Jesus spoke to her that it was not her fault. He repeated it over and over, like a beautiful melody. It sang deep into her heart. She was free to live.

Romans 8:31-32 – If God is for us, who can ever be against us? Since He did not spare even His own Son but gave Him up for us all, won't He also give us everything else?

JAMES' STORY:

James was sad, he had always been sad. He had an older brother, a sister and a mom who was in deep depression. His mom cried all the time, day and night. His father was not a part of their lives. His mother met another man who was abusive. She fled and her despair multiplied. The family was very dysfunctional. His mom started drinking. The house was filthy. James remembers being ridiculed for being poor. He felt all alone.

At age nine, James got a new stepdad, a good role model. James found his mom's personal journal and discovered that his biological father had been sentenced to jail for eight years for sexually molesting his sister. He detested his father. When James was age twelve, his step dad left. James began drinking in order to bury his own feelings and began a life of alcohol and sex. At age sixteen, he was using and selling drugs. He was eighteen years old when he ended up in jail. James was twenty-one when his mother died.

When James went back to his childhood memories, he remembered his mom's sadness. The family was sad. Anger welled up. He was angry at his mom for not being his hero, angry at God, just angry – angry at everyone. Anger and sadness. Sadness and anger. These two emotions acted like a tag team.

For James, sadness was acceptable. Everyone closest to him was unhappy and depressed. Sadness connected him to his mom, being sad honoured her by empathizing with her. It was James' encounter with the presence of Jesus, during one of his Inner Healing sessions, that the door to freedom began to open. Hope entered.

James went back to the memory of himself as a little boy, sitting by his mom's bed. Her tears were flowing. Life felt out of control. He now sensed Jesus in this memory, speaking tenderly into his soul. Jesus said that his mom's sadness was not his fault and there was nothing that this little boy could have done. He was loved. He was not alone. Jesus was with him. James was relieved, yet his sadness still lingered. It was up to James to choose:

- keep the sadness
- give the sadness to Jesus

Jesus was waiting for James to give it to Him. And James did.

James is now vibrantly free of all that heavy sadness. His heart is on fire for Jesus. He is presently attending Bible College. Lately, he has been thinking of his biological dad, hoping to connect with him to tell him that he is forgiven, tell him that Jesus loves him. All his sadness is gone and James is excited about life. Jesus has taken his hand.

Psalm 30:11-12 – You have turned my mourning into joyful dancing. You have taken away my clothes of mourning and clothed me with joy, that I might sing praises to you and not be silent. O Lord my God, I will give you thanks forever.

HOLLY'S STORY

Holly, age eight, was told to do the dishes. She was in the midst of her chore when she decided to go to the washroom. When she came out, her father was in the hall, his eyes filled her with terror. Because of her fear, she wet her pants, then placed the blame on herself. Shame flooded her tiny being. It felt like Jesus was not there. Holly felt so alone for nobody cared, and no one treasured her.

When Holly went back into her memory, she sensed an angel hovering above her, in the hall. Jesus spoke to her saying, "I love you even if your dad doesn't. I will never leave you nor abandon you."

In her mind, Holly saw Jesus and she wanted to run into His arms but did not know if He really wanted her. She timidly moved towards Him and sat on his lap, wondering if this could be forever.

Jesus replied, "Yes, my love is forever." She gave her anger to Jesus and forgave her dad. Peace came into her heart. Now the memory was comforting, relaxing and full of joy. Jesus loved her; the fear was gone.

Psalm 13:5-6 – I trust in your unfailing love. I will rejoice because you have rescued me. I will sing to the Lord because He is good to me.

RONALD'S STORY:

Ronald was the oldest child in his family, and given a lot of responsibilities. His dad was critical of him, making fun of him in front of his friends. Everything Ronald did was wrong. He was verbally and physically abused by his dad who also abused his mom. That made Ronald angry. The kids at school abused him, called him an 'Indian', degrading him. His anger gave him purpose and energy.

At the young age of twelve, Ronald's dad told him that he was going to be just like his uncle – a bad influence. At age thirteen, Ronald was forced from the house to live alone in the holiday trailer. He felt unwanted. By age fifteen, he was drinking heavily and it felt so good. It was a great escape from his pain. Ronald became a well-known wrestler; others respected him. He was no longer bullied. On the outside he had power – on the inside was anger.

By mid-life, Ronald had destroyed his marriage, lost his driver's license, and family. He did not see his children grow up, nor his grandchildren. He did not go to his mother's funeral because he was drunk. Jesus talked to Ronald about his anger, telling him to give it to Him, and release his dad into His hands. When Ronald gave his anger to Jesus, he felt free of the heaviness. Ronald decided to forgive himself for a whole list of sins he had committed against himself, others, and God.

Ronald forgave himself for wasting so many years. Jesus was beside him, loving him dearly – always had and always will.

2 Corinthians 4:8-9 – We are pressed on every side by troubles, but we are not crushed. We are perplexed, but not driven to despair. We are hunted down, but never abandoned by God. We get knocked down but we are not destroyed.

CATHY'S STORY:

Cathy was sexually abused as a little girl, by her grandfather. The abuse began when she was very young, up until age eight. Her grandfather threatened her. Cathy felt dirty. She was very confused. Her trust was broken.

It was after her grandfather died that Cathy was able to face her pain. After one of her Inner Healing Sessions, Cathy opened the door to her own healing by writing her thoughts in a letter to her grandfather:

"It took me longer than it should have to get this off my chest, but you need to understand that what you have done has not only hurt me, but it had control over my life and affected every aspect in it. Not only have I lost all trust and hope in other people, including relationships and friendships, but you also stole my childhood because of what happened. I avoid thinking about my childhood because it reminds me of the trauma I experienced. I had to learn to block out so many memories in order to function and I would have to say the worst part is having nobody to talk to while I was growing up, which led me to believe I was creating my own pain and using it as an excuse to use(drugs). I never used to believe you were the reason I had started my addiction, but now that I got all the information, it makes sense. The pain I covered up was always there and drinking numbed it and created temporary happiness. Perhaps the unhappiness I

experienced so long was the reason I enjoyed the feeling of being under the influence because it was creating the person I strived to be, examples are being confident, not having any fears and being able to talk about my feelings. You being gone makes it harder for me to express how I fell but honestly do believe in my heart I am able, and I do forgive you for the wrongs you have done in my life, not only for you, but in order for me to move forward in life. I need to move on and learn to let people in and let myself be loved. With all being said, I have chosen to give my remaining hurt and anger to God. He is the only One who has the ability to do so. As much hurt you have caused, I always have and I always will have love for you. I also love myself enough to take this step and let myself heal. I am don't feeling hurt and controlled by the past. It's time to live. As much as I allowed this to have power over me, I promise I will fight even harder in my recovery."

2 Corinthians 1:8-10 – We were crushed and overwhelmed beyond our ability to endure, and we thought we would never live through it. In fact, we expected to die. But as a result, we stopped relying on ourselves and learned to rely only on God who raises the dead. And He did rescue us from mortal danger and He will rescue us again. We have placed our confidence in Him, and He will continue to rescue us.

VICKI'S STORY:

At age three, Vicki was taken from her grandparents' house to be with her mom. Intense fear invaded her soul for her mom's presence intimidated her.

Vicki was locked in her room with nothing but her mattress, a dresser, and her cat. Her mom preferred the company of a man, blaming her daughter for ruining her life.

Vicki felt trapped and powerless. While alone in her room, Jesus called to her. She sensed that Jesus was safe.

As a child and throughout her growing up years, men were given power to sexually abuse her. Her mother did not care. She cursed Vicki. It tore Vicki's heart to be used as a piece of meat. Jesus spoke to this fragile girl saying, "I will protect you. I love you and will save you." He was beside her, giving her strength to carry on, taking the pain with her, feeling the hurt with her. Jesus held Vicki. Peace and respect flowed over her. Jesus put a beautiful armour upon her, protecting her arms, legs, chest and head. It was not heavy. Jesus declared, "You are my warrior. You are filled with my Spirit."

Vicki forgave her mom for demonstrating the power of sex and money, her way of overcoming pain. She forgave her mom because her mom did not know what she was doing, then put her mom into God's hands. He can deal with her. Vicki blessed her mom, praying that one day her mom will know God for herself.

Vicki also forgave her mom's boyfriend. She had hated him and now chose to let go of the anger. It was no longer hers to hang on to. Jesus told her that she was important to Him, that He had died for her. Jesus was for her, not against her. She felt secure and safe. Vicki's mother's sins were not hers anymore and Vicki's sins will not be passed onto her daughters. The destructive cycle was broken. Vicki was free to live her own life now.

Vicki had another memory. When she was seventeen years old, she remembered her mom angrily spitting out the words, "I brought you into this world and I can take you out! You're going to be just like me, a failure!"

Jesus was there and asked her to give Him the pain.

PRAYER – in dealing with a curse:

In the name of Jesus, I renounce/reverse what was spoken and break the vow/curse of (name it) that was made against me by (person who spoke the words) and I declare it null, having no power, and void, nothing remains, in the name of Jesus. Instead of these cursed words, I receive God's words of blessing that (opposite of the curse). I open my heart for Jesus to pour His love into it. Thank you, dear Jesus! And I forgive this person because they didn't know what they were doing. I put them in your hands, Jesus. In Jesus' name. Amen.

Throughout Vicki's years of sexual abuse, there were times when men spoke endearing words to her, which made her feel special and loved, yet deep inside, she felt worthless. Having sex with those men also gave her a sense of power over them.

I talked to her regarding soul ties, a deep emotional connection between two people, which is created by sexual interaction, consensual or non-consensual. When God created Adam and Eve, His plan was for them to be joined together as one in marriage.[158] When husband and wife respect the hallowedness of their commitment to each other, a healthy soul tie is formed. When a man or woman have sexual relationships outside of marriage, they too are bound, united as one. A powerful unhealthy soul tie is formed, a tie that keeps pulling them together.

I Corinthians 6:16 – And don't you realize that if a man joins himself to a prostitute, he becomes one body with her? For the Scriptures say, "The two are united into one."

Life can be compared to a puzzle, with many pieces. When a soul tie transpires, we give some of our life pieces to the other person and receive some of theirs. Without marriage, their pieces do not fit into our puzzle and some of our pieces have

---

[158] Genesis 2:24

164

been given away. We are confused, our life puzzle is not making sense.

Vicki made a list of men, who had either abused her or she had abused – forty-four in all. In the name of Jesus, she has the authority to break those soul ties supernaturally. Vicki prayed the prayer of breaking her soul ties, she went through her list one by one.

PRAYER – in breaking soul ties:
In the name of Jesus, I break the soul tie between (name) and myself. All the pieces that belong to me are to come back to me, and all the pieces that belong to (name) are to go back to (name), and the soul tie is to be supernaturally broken in the name of Jesus. I ask you God, to remove all ungodly influences of (name any visual pictures, thoughts, words, feelings, etc), I give them all to You, to hold for me, I don't want them anymore. Make me whole again and set me free to live my life. Thank you, dear Jesus! In Jesus' name, Amen.

Vicki had five miscarriages, some tubal pregnancies and, at age twenty-one, she had an abortion. She felt angry at herself for not fighting for her baby's life. Vicki was angry because she was an alcoholic and druggie, and lost the right to parent her two daughters. Her soul was like a dark cave. She asked God for forgiveness and chose to forgive herself for the abortion. Now the anger is gone, there is a rock in the cave's door of her soul, with Jesus standing guard. She no longer needs to live in that darkness.

During Vicki's dark time, she mutilated herself, on her forearm, resulting in a long line of stitches, a life-long reminder of what she had done. Jesus understand her for He too, has scars and had His journey of pain. He understands her pain. He held her, comforting her.

I would love to end Vicki's story by stating that she is walking a road of freedom from her past but she is not there yet. She has moved on from the treatment program, trying to maintain sobriety. It is an intense struggle and holds many challenges. Jesus is beside her in this long road of recovery and freedom. Someday, she hopes to write her dramatic story for all to read.

Vicki is a warrior, fighting her way through life. She now has Jesus at her side. She is His treasure, His princess. Always has been, always will be.

Daniel 10:19 – "Don't be afraid," He said, "for you are very precious to God. Peace! Be encouraged! Be strong!"

Inner healing is a journey which continues throughout each of our lives. Unless we own our pain and bring it to Jesus, He is not able to bring healing. When we expose our wounds to the Healer, He eagerly speaks truth, resulting in a deep peace. Jesus is in our pain: past, present, and future. He is with us all the time. He understands pain; He is our Healer.

You will know the truth
and the truth will set you free. . . .
If the Son sets you free, you are truly free.
– John 8:32,36

REFLECTIONS: Chapter 11 – Their stories

1. Which life story can you relate to?
2. How does Jesus transform pain into peace?
3. How can a curse be transformed into a blessing?
4. You have the authority to break an unhealthy soul tie.
   Is there anyone you need to break a soul tie with and also forgive?
5. Be patient with your journey of healing.
   It takes time.
   Jesus understands.
   He is with you.

Notes & Journaling:

People have often asked me how I am able to listen to such painful stories. The following writing is my response:

Into His Arms

At times, I am overwhelmed.
So much cruelty in this world.
Children robbed of their purity.
Women beaten into submission.
Men spewing anger as lava from the mountain top.
Who am I to believe
that there is any hope of goodness?

I look around.
My eyes rest upon the face of Jesus.
I gaze into His eyes, so full of compassion,
a 'knowing' of what pain is.
He calls me to His side,
- and I run to Him.

Peace oozes into my being.
It is gentle,
like the fragrant scent of a blushing rose
carried by a sunlit breeze.
It is powerful.
Slowly it overtakes the darkness.
I let it flow into the inner chambers of my heart.
Peace, sweet peace.

My heart is still.
It beats life.
It reaches out to touch each bleeding soul
in tenderness.
Placing them into my Father's arms.
-author IRene Hamm

Chapter 12

Inviting Jesus' Presence

We need Jesus in our life. He understands our heart and thoughts. He loves us deeply. His truth will set us free.[159] Life can hold many hardships: heartbreak, illness, injury, death and abandonment. When we have been viciously knocked down by life's events, go to Jesus. He is waiting for you.

Jesus is with each of us:
- every moment
- day and night
- everywhere
- always

Pain demands attention: it needs to be acknowledged and embraced before we can move on. Exposing our pain to Healer Jesus, and receiving His truth, brings freedom.

There are many emotions that you may feel as you work through the verses.
- Helpless: unable to defend oneself or to act without help
- Hopeless: feeling or causing despair about something, no solution
- Powerless: without ability, influence, or power
- Alone: having no one to turn to
- Not good enough: lacking the quality or quantity required, inadequate
- Unacceptable: not satisfactory or supported
- Rejected: cast out, do not belong

---

[159] John 8:32

- Worthless: having no value
- Abandoned: discarded, deserted, or cast off
- Abused: treated with cruelty and/or violence
- Anxiety: lack of control, unpredictable, overwhelmed
- Betrayed: broken trust, disloyalty
- Confused: unable to make sense, cannot think clearly
- Depressed: hopeless, defeated, helpless
- Filthy: unable to have worth, marked as dirty
- Sadness: lingering sorrow, like a dark cloud
- False guilt: it is your fault, hopeless in correcting
- True guilt: have committed an offense (Chapters 6 & 7)
- Anger: emotional response to an injustice (Chapter 8)

Steps to healing from pain:
- Validate your pain. Accept it and own your emotions. What are you feeling?
- Follow the pain back to a memory, the first time you felt it. What happened?
- Explore the memory. What feels true?
- Know that Jesus is in the memory with you.

Sense His presence.
- Ask Jesus, "What does He want you to know?"
- Receive His truth and peace.
- Check the memory – does your previous belief still feel true?
- If there is pain left in the memory, feel it, and ask Jesus what is true.

The following verses address woundedness. Follow through the steps to receive healing from Jesus.

FEELING WEARY

Matthew 11:28 - Come to Me, all of you who are weary and carry heavy burdens and I will give you rest.

1. What are the heavy burdens that you are carrying? Responsibilities? Obligations? People's expectations?
2. How does it make you feel as you carry them?
3. See Jesus with you.
   Close your eyes and see Him.
   Where is He? Can you sense Him?
   Look at Him.
4. What does He want you to do with your burdens?
5. What do you want to do with them?
6. Jesus, is there to hear anything that You may want to say?

Read the verse again. Receive His rest.

_____

_____

_____

_____

_____

_____

_____

_____

_____

_____

_____

_____

_____

_____

FEELING ALONE

James 4:8 - Come close to God, and God will come close to you.

1. Close your eyes and see yourself all alone.
2. Go back to a childhood memory where you first felt all alone. Where were you? What happened?
3. Jesus says that He has never left you, He is right there with you. Can you see Him, sense Him?
4. Is there anything blocking you from seeing Him? Anger? Unforgiveness? Guilt?
5. Bring it to Jesus. Give it to Him.
6. What is your heart feeling?
7. Jesus is there. Do you want to ask Him something?
8. Let Him hold you and fill your heart with His love.

Read the verse again. Receive His presence beside you.

_____

_____

_____

_____

_____

_____

_____

_____

_____

_____

_____

_____

_____

_____

_____

_____

_____

Jeremiah 31:3 - I have loved you . . . with an everlasting love. With unfailing love, I have drawn you to myself. -

1. What does it feel like to be unlovable?
2. Do you have a memory that comes to mind, as a child, where you felt unlovable? How did it make you feel?
3. Where are you in the memory?
4. Close your eyes. Where is Jesus in that memory?
5. Can you see His face?
   Lift up your eyes to look into His eyes.
6. Jesus, what do You want this little child to know?

Read the verse again.

Open your heart and let His love completely fill it.

_____
_____
_____
_____
_____
_____
_____
_____
_____
_____
_____
_____
_____
_____
_____
_____
_____
_____
_____
_____

FEELING LOST

Psalm 32:8 - I will guide you along the best pathway for your life. I will advise you and watch over you.

1. What does it feel like to be uncertain in your life path?
2. Which memory comes to mind as you feel this 'lostness'?
3. What is going on around you? Where are you?
4. Close your eyes and look for Jesus. Can you see Him?
5. Ask for His guidance.
6. Jesus, what do you want this person to know?
7. Is there anything that this person needs to do right now?

Read the verse again.
Receive the truth that He will guide and advise you.

_____

_____

_____

_____

_____

_____

_____

_____

_____

_____

_____

_____

_____

_____

_____

_____

FEELING UNWANTED

Psalm 27:8 - My heart has heard you say, "Come and talk with Me." And my heart responds, "Lord, I am coming."

1. Do you have a longing in your heart to be wanted? What does it feel like?
2. Is there a memory that comes to mind when you are feeling unwanted?
3. Where were you in the memory?
4. What were you longing for?
5. Close your eyes and look around in the memory. Can you sense and see Jesus with you?
6. He wants you to come and talk with Him. Choose to go to Him.
7. Jesus, what do you want this person to know?

Read the verse again. Welcome Jesus' Presence.

_____

_____

_____

_____

_____

_____

_____

_____

_____

_____

_____

_____

_____

_____

_____

FEELING ABANDONED

Psalm 27:10 - Even if my father and mother abandon me, the Lord will hold me close.

1. As a child, when did you feel abandoned?
2. What does it feel like?
3. When was the first time you felt abandoned?
4. Where were you when it happened?
5. Close your eyes and sense Jesus. What is He doing?
6. Jesus, what do you want this person to know?
7. How do you see this person, dear Jesus?
8. Is there anyone that needs to be forgiven?
   Forgive them for they did not know what they were doing.
9. Jesus, is there anything else that you want to say?

Read the verse again. Receive His deep love for you.

_____

_____

_____

_____

_____

_____

_____

_____

_____

_____

_____

_____

_____

_____

_____

_____

FEELING TOO BUSY

Psalm 46:10 - Be still, and know that I am God.

1. What is making you busy? What are your responsibilities?
2. Feel the weight of your activities.
   What does it feel like?
3. Invite Jesus to go with you into your busyness.
   Sit down with Him. Breathe. Be still.
4. Jesus, is there anything that You want to say?
5. What do You want to do with all their busyness?
6. Is there anything that they need to change?
   If so, what?
7. What do they need to do to be still with you?
8. How much do you love them, Jesus?

Read the verse again. Be still. Rest in Him.

_____

_____

_____

_____

_____

_____

_____

_____

_____

_____

_____

_____

_____

_____

_____

_____

FEELING FEAR

Psalm 56:3 - When I am afraid, I will put my trust in you.

1. What are you afraid of?
   A person, some event, your future, yourself?
2. What does your fear feel like?
   Vulnerable, helpless, powerless, unsafe, alone?
3. As you feel it, what memory comes to mind?
   When was the first time you felt this fear?
4. Where are you and what is happening?
5. Close your eyes.
   Can you see Jesus in that memory? What is He doing?
6. Jesus, is there anything You want to say to this person?
7. Give Jesus your fears.

Read the verse again.

Receive the truth of His trustworthiness.

_____
_____
_____
_____
_____
_____
_____
_____
_____
_____
_____
_____
_____
_____
_____

FEELING BROKEN-HEARTED

Psalm 147:3 - He heals the broken-hearted and bandages their wounds.

1. What does your heart feel like when it is broken?
2. What has shattered your heart?
3. Close your eyes. See all the pieces of your heart. What are you feeling as you look at them?
4. Look around to see Jesus. Do you sense Him?
5. Jesus, what do you want to do with all these pieces?
6. Watch Him as He bandages your wounds. What does it feel like?
7. What does Jesus want to say as He bandages your wounds?

Read the verse again. Receive His healing.

_____
_____
_____
_____
_____
_____
_____
_____
_____
_____
_____
_____
_____
_____
_____
_____
_____
_____

FEELING GUILT

Isaiah 1:18 - "Come now, let's settle this," says the Lord. "Though your sins are like scarlet, I will make them as white as snow. Though they are red like crimson, I will make them as white as wool."

1. What do you feel guilty for?
2. What does your guilt look like?
   Jesus says that your guilt is like scarlet, crimson in color. See your guilt that way. It is vibrant. A huge stain.
3. Where is Jesus? Look at Him. Look into His eyes.
4. Ask Jesus what can you can do with this guilt.
5. Ask Him if there is anything that He wants you to know regarding your guilt?
6. Give Jesus your guilt. What does He do with it?
7. How does that make you feel?

Read the verse again. Receive His forgiveness.
Let Him wash you white as snow.

FEELING SADNESS

Psalm 42:11 - Why am I discouraged? Why is my heart so sad? I will put my hope in God! I will praise Him again, my Saviour and my God.

1. Why is there sadness within you? When did it begin?
2. Feel it. Close your eyes. Go to the memory where the sadness began. Where are you in the memory?
3. Look for Jesus. Where is He?
4. Is there anything that Jesus wants to say to you about your sadness?
5. Is there a reason why you keep this sadness?
   Do you want to keep it?
6. Give Jesus your sadness.
7. Let Him fill your heart with His love until it overflows.

Read the verse again. Receive His hope and joy.

_____
_____
_____
_____
_____
_____
_____
_____
_____
_____
_____
_____
_____
_____
_____

FEELING HOPELESS

Psalms 94:19 - When doubts filled my mind, your comfort gave me renewed hope and cheer.

1. What thoughts of doubt fill your mind?
2. How do those thoughts make you feel?
3. What is going on in your life? How does that feel?
4. Follow the emotions back to a memory in your childhood. What happened in that memory? What are you feeling?
5. Where are you in the memory? Who is there?
6. Close your eyes and look for Jesus. Where is He? Do you sense Him there?
7. Go to Him and look in His face.
8. What does Jesus want to speak to you, for you to know?

Read the verse again. Receive His comfort and cheer.

_____

_____

_____

_____

_____

_____

_____

_____

_____

_____

_____

_____

_____

_____

_____

FEELING WEAK

Deuteronomy 31:6 - So be strong and courageous! Do not be afraid and do not panic before them. For the Lord your God will personally go ahead of you. He will neither fail you nor abandon you.

1. What does it feel like to be weak?
2. Feel your emotions and follow them all the way back when you were a child.
   What happened in that memory? Where were you?
3. Why did you feel weak?
4. Close your eyes.
   Where is Jesus in that memory? Can you sense Him?
5. Run to Him. What does Jesus want to say to you?

Read the verse again. Receive strength and courage from Him.

_____
_____
_____
_____
_____
_____
_____
_____
_____
_____
_____
_____
_____
_____
_____
_____

Chapter 13

My Reality

This is the toughest chapter for me to write, not because it exposes my personal deep pain, but because it was an immense challenge trying to effectively illuminate my experience of the presence of Jesus. I can relate to the man in John 9, who was healed of blindness. The religious leaders flooded him with questions in their effort to prove that Jesus was a phony, that this Healer was a sinner, causing havoc within the security of their religion. The religious leaders demanded to know how the blind man was healed.

John 9:25 - "I don't know whether he is a sinner," the man replied. "But I know this: I was blind and now I can see!"

This chapter is my story, my experience. I know that the presence of Jesus is real, for I have felt His closeness and heard Him many, many times. It is not a conjuring up of His presence, nor a type of trickery of the mind, His presence is and was real. Sometimes His voice speaks into my thoughts when I listen for Him, other times He speaks when I am not thinking about Him. At times, I have felt His hand touch my hair in affection. I have smelled the fragrance of His presence – sweet and tender.

When I become mindful of Him, I sense His presence wherever I may be. In the same way as the radio dial connects me to the sound waves of a radio station, so does the dial of my soul allow me to connect with the reality of His presence. He was always near. He is always with me.

We are all unique, there is no one else like you, nobody like me. And every person's relationship with Jesus is one of a kind. We are created differently. We are individuals and have individual interactions with Jesus that coincide with who we are, and what is meaningful to each of us.

I have known the loving presence of Jesus many times throughout my life. My personal interaction with Him began during my high school years, going through the challenges of being a teenager. I often escaped to the last row of trees on our farm, climbed up onto a branch, and talked to Jesus. I knew that He heard me.

My need of His presence intensified when I give birth to my daughter Cherie, my second child, on May 11, 1981. She was born blind and, at seven months, my husband and I were told that she had cerebral palsy; part of her brain that controlled movement was damaged. I really needed God.

Cherie under-went several surgeries, the first one at ten days old, then, at two months, she had eye and bladder surgery. Cherie had three seizures after the last two operations.

"My baby, what is happening to my baby?" I loved her so much. In answer to my question, Jesus spoke into my mind saying that He loved her too; much more than I ever could. He was there with me as I cried. He was holding both of us. His peace washed over my soul.

Journaling became my way of processing what was happening. As I journaled, telling God my woes, He spoke to me, telling me that He heard me. He held me. He became my Anchor, my Comfort, and my Joy.

Psalm 55:17 – Morning, noon, and night I cry out in my distress, and the Lord hears my voice.

Before Cherie's birth, I did not realize the incredible gift this baby was going to be. I had no idea that she would be born

188

with malformed eyes and have cerebral palsy, that her body would become weaker over time. I had no idea how rich my life would be because of her disability. But Jesus did. He filled me with His presence as I chose to trust in Him. Looking back on the thirty-six and one-half years of her life, I am very grateful to have had her.

My faith was challenged over her lifetime; my life held great joy and great sorrow. The hardest days of my life were the final twenty-six days of Cherie's life while she was in the hospital. It was an emotional roller coaster. Some of those days I believed that she was going to get better, other days it felt like she was going to die. They were my darkest days, and at the same time, the most vibrant and powerful.

Isaiah 45:3 - "I will give you treasures hidden in the darkness – secret riches. I will do this so that you may know that I am the Lord, the God of Israel, the One who calls you by name."

Throughout those days, while Cherie was in the hospital, her constantly changing medical status had my emotions on a roller coaster. She appeared as though she was dying one hour, then bringing hope of recovery the next.

I journaled a lot. I was so very tired, but I just had to express my emotions and thoughts to God. Journaling helped me process my reality; it stabilized my soul, anchoring it on the Rock. Even if life did not make sense, God's presence filled me with His peace. He stilled the raging storm within my soul and breathed a calmness into its depth. There was a quietness within His presence. Day after day, in the hospital, Jesus' presence was felt in spectacular ways.

On the second day of Cherie's hospital stay, she told me that she had a rough night due to leg spasms. She had asked God if He could please take her to heaven. He responded – "Soon!" When she told me this, I wondered, how soon is 'soon'? I realized that my peace did not depend on an answer but was only possible by believing that He cared. He held me close, quieting my fears.

Psalm 34:4 – I prayed to the Lord, and He answered me. He freed me from all my fears.

One day, at the beginning of her hospital stay, Cherie was doing poorly. I cried as I held her tightly; I was afraid she was going to die. Cherie consoled me. "God is in charge, it's okay."

I chose to believe that God was trustworthy in the midst of life's instability. He was the only Anchor available. Jesus was right beside me. Peace once more flowed into my soul.

Psalm 91:1 – Whoever dwells in the shelter of the Most High will rest in the shadow of the Almighty. I will say of the Lord, "He is my refuge and my fortress, my God, in whom I trust."

Cherie was taken for an ultrasound of her liver and an echocardiogram of her heart. She had to lie flat for this procedure, causing her body tremendous stress. Her breathing was laboured and spasms overtook her legs. My heart was overcome with deep sorrow as I wiped her forehead with a wet washcloth. She persevered in her pain. Jesus was beside me, giving me strength and pouring His peace into my being. He calmed my soul.

There were days when Cherie felt better. I was greatly relieved, and very tired. I loved picking Cherie's brain, exploring her understanding of life. She had a unique relationship with God. So, at the end of the first week of her stay in the hospital, I recorded our discussion on my phone, unbeknown to her. I asked her what she would like everyone to know.

"Before I die?" she asked.

"Yes, before you die."

We discussed death so calmly. She spoke of heaven, and of trusting God; He never let her down. Three weeks later, this video was shown at her funeral. It is accessible on YouTube under 'Cherie Hamm's Interview on Life & Heaven'.

Another medical procedure was performed. A PICC line was inserted into the vein of her right bicep and threaded to her heart, making it easier to administer medications. Even though she had to lie flat on her back while it was performed, Cherie was calm, stating that Jesus was standing right beside her during the procedure, telling her that she was okay. Her body and mind fully relaxed.

Psalm 91:4 – He will cover you with His feathers, and under His wings you will find refuge; His faithfulness will be your shield and rampart.

One day, I saw the family doctor at the nurses' station, just as I was leaving Cherie's room. I really wanted to speak with him. I waited in the hallway, but he went the other direction. I wondered if I should wait for him. How long would he be? God reminded me that He, not the doctor, is the Healer, so I could leave Cherie in His hands. I left for work without speaking to the doctor. It was okay. I chose to trust God.

Later in the evening I went to Cherie's condo to pack her things, so she could move into a unit with nursing care. It did not feel like she was going back home for I feared she would never get better. How could I live without her? What will my life be like without my daughter? I loved her deeply. My heart was so very sad. Please God! Then I heard the words that Cherie had spoken to me, "God is in charge. Trust Him." I breathed in His peace.

On day eleven, Cherie had a respiratory crisis. I was sure that she was dying. I spoke to her, believing that she was breathing her last. I found myself coaching her to go, to leave this world, if Jesus was calling her. I could not believe what I just said – just go? I felt Jesus' presence, giving me courage to speak release to Cherie. That evening Cherie had another respiratory crisis, then began to breathe once more. It was hard dealing with the haunting presence of death so very close, but the presence of Jesus overtook it.

That night I decided to sleep in her hospital room. I woke up at 3 a.m. because I thought I heard Cherie calling to me. But when I stood beside her bed, she was peacefully sleeping. Seconds later, the oxygen hose separated from her mask. I reconnected it and went back to bed. In the morning, I realized that Jesus had awoken me to reconnect the oxygen tube. I had sensed the presence of Jesus, taking care of her, tending to her needs. He was the One in control.

Psalm 121:5 – The Lord Himself watches over you! The Lord stands beside you as your protective shade.

I had many questions and no answers. I was emotionally exhausted. I went home to play the piano, expressing my wounded heart and Jesus tenderly soothed my soul. His peace flooded over my being. He held my heart in His gentle love. He was trustworthy.

On day fourteen, Cherie was much more talkative and hungrier. My heart jumped for joy, not realizing it was the steroids that caused her appetite to re-surface. The doctor delivered the good news that Cherie was out of her critical state and recovering. I was delighted, but deep inside I felt her life was still in the balance.

Later, it was suspected Cherie had some hemorrhaging in her lungs. That evening, the doctor arranged for Cherie to be flown to a larger city hospital. I went with her. The medivac flight was smooth. I looked out of the plane window, into the deep dark sky filled with hundreds of twinkling stars. It was so very peaceful. The Creator was with us, encapsulating our souls.

Psalm 8:3-5 – When I look at the night sky and see the work of your fingers – the moon and the stars you set in place – what are people that you should think about them, mere mortals that you should care for them? Yet you made them only a little lower than God and crowned them with glory and honour.

Our arrival, at the University city hospital, was completed in record time. Cherie was passive and cooperative as she endured all sorts of testing and prodding. The specialist came in to tell her that she may die because she had blood clots in her lungs. She responded by saying that she was not afraid of dying.

The doctors did what they could. A morphine routine was started to deal with her leg spasms and difficulty in breathing. Death appeared to be coming closer.

In my darkest hours, I listened to a song, a duet of *Oceans* (regarding walking into the deep waters) and *You Make Me Brave.*[160] My soul heaved with deep grief. Sorrow roared from the chasm of pain, exploded as a geyser from deep within. The pain of losing Cherie, overwhelmed and suffocated my soul. I knew that I could not carry the extremely devastating reality of my daughter dying, it was too crushing.

Psalm 61:1-4 – O God, listen to my cry! Hear my prayer! From the ends of the earth, I cry to you for help when my heart is overwhelmed. Lead me to the towering rock of safety, for you are my safe refuge, a fortress where my enemies cannot reach me. Let me live forever in your sanctuary, safe beneath the shelter of your wings!

---

[160] *You make me Brave* & *Oceans* sung by Caleb & Kelsey Cover

I entered Jesus' presence and took shelter in His arms. He knew how to calm the raging waves within my soul. I sensed that I was in His pocket, hiding in His being. The storm was swirling vehemently around me but I was safe. Jesus' presence surrounded me. It was peaceful. I rested in Him.

Psalm 107:28-29 – "Lord, help!" they cried in their trouble, and He saved them from their distress. He calmed the storm to a whisper and stilled the waves.

Cherie's health was declining. On Day twenty-five, I read Psalm 23 to her. Verse 4 became very real to me – 'Even when I walk through the darkest valley, I will not be afraid, for You are close beside me. Your rod and Your staff protect and comfort me.'

That evening, Cherie had phlegm in her throat and could not speak clearly. I could not understand her. At 3 a.m., Cherie's feeble voice woke me, asking me to bend her knee in order to relax the leg spasm. As I sat at the end of her bed, the sweet aroma of a Stargazer Lily filled the room. I knew it was the fragrance of God's tender presence in our midst.

The next morning, Cherie's voice was weak but the phlegm was gone, I could understand her. I offered grateful praise to my Father.

The doctor came in and offered two options:
- continue medications in order to sustain life.
- discontinue the medication, give her a morphine drip for comfort, and allow her body to go through its process of dying.

Cherie agreed to the morphine option.

That same day, on November 4th, 2017, day twenty-six in the hospital, at 5:58 p.m., Cherie left this earth. She was gone. An amazing peace surrounded her. My daughter was so beautiful, at peace in the arms of Jesus. This memory calmed my many overwhelming future sorrows.

Psalm 116:15 – The Lord cares deeply when His loved ones die.

Oh, the presence of Jesus! There is nothing that can compare to it. He dwells in the innermost chambers of the soul. It cannot be swayed by life's situations. Jesus' presence breathes life; it holds a deep peace.

- He loves me.
- He loves you.
- He loves all of us - intensely.

SELAH - pause with me.

After Cherie died, I compiled my journal entries into a book, 'Her Last 26 Days on Earth'. It gives witness of the richness of Jesus' presence during her hospital stay. My journaling demonstrated what trusting God looked like, and revealed the character of a trustworthy God. His presence is precious.

PRAYER:
Oh Lord, I need You. I want to trust you. My life seems out of control at times. I chose to trust in You. Hold me tight. Don't let me go. Speak into my need of You. In Jesus' name. Amen.

I have carried you before you were born.

I will be your God throughout your lifetime –

until your hair is white with age.

I made you, and I will care for you.

I will carry you along and save you.

-Isaiah 46:3-4

REFLECTIONS: Chapter 13 – My Reality

1. How have you experienced Jesus?
2. Does it feel true that Jesus has always loved you deeply?
3. In what area of your life do you want Jesus' peace?
4. Come and trust Jesus. He is right beside you. Talk to Him. Listen for Him.
5. How do you view death?
6. Trust Him with your loved ones, your hopes, and dreams, your future, and your life.

Notes & Journaling:

_____
_____
_____
_____
_____
_____
_____
_____
_____
_____
_____
_____
_____
_____
_____
_____
_____
_____
_____
_____

Chapter 14

Grieving with Jesus

Grief refers to loss. When we talk about grief, we immediately think of physical death, but there are many deep griefs that our souls mourn:

- the termination of a relationship
- losing a job, a home, or prized possession
- deterioration of health and independence
- destruction of self image or status in life

Sometimes we do not recognize the immensity of grief outside of death. All grief takes time to heal, and it is an individual journey.

Grief causes time to stand still. We become numb, unable to process what has happened – seemingly there is no visible pathway before us. We find ourselves in unknown territory, and we do not know how to live in this unfamiliar state.

Our souls desperately look for stability in life, something to cling to, for the storm has brought immense devastation. Nothing is the same, life has changed irreversibly. We cry out for an anchor in this desolate, raging storm of life.

In my storm of grief, I chose to believe that Jesus was trustworthy. There was no one else to look to. I kept looking into His eyes and He comforted me. He knew what was happening. He assured me that I would make it, as I tightly clung to Him.

John 14:27 – I am leaving you with a gift – peace of mind and heart. And the peace I give is a gift the world cannot give. So, don't be troubled or afraid.

Grief visited me often during the life of my daughter, Cherie. I grieved her blindness, her inability to see what I visually enjoyed. Her cerebral palsy limited her mobility, causing restrictions to enjoy what I took pleasure in. Other children, my daughter's age, hit milestones which were impossible for Cherie to achieve. Many times, my heart was grief-stricken. I mourned. Then she died, leaving me behind on this earth.

Grief holds many deep emotions; it is bottomless with no boundaries. It flows wherever it so chooses. Sometimes it flows as calm waters, and sometimes it billows as a waterfall pummelling over the cliff edge. Our minds try to comprehend and grasp the reality which comes with the loss in our life. A void is present where once there was joy and satisfaction.

Nothing can equip us for the unrestricted sorrow that takes over our souls when a loss is experienced. A hole surrounds our soul. We somehow need to live with this emptiness, in our present day, and all our days to come. Nobody truly understands the depth of our grief. Our grief is individual. Everyone has different circumstances and their own uniqueness concerning their loss.

There are many variables that determine grief:
- age – yours and whoever else was involved
- previous life experiences
- the reason for the loss
- how it happened
- if it was expected or not
- your relationship with what was lost
- your last experience with it/them.

There are various possibilities of each factor, along with a magnitude of conceivable combinations. Grief is unique for each person.

Grief is a journey of soul-sucking waves, which over time, do become less frequent, less turbulent. Grief can be compared to the weather – sometimes the skies are sunny, sometimes it is cloudy, and sometimes there are torrential downpours of sorrow.

In the days when my soul desperately cried out, I turned to God and I clung to Him, with all the energy that I could muster. He alone understood my grief. He was beside me and knew my heart. He grasped me tightly in His arms and held me close to His heart. His comfort was a balm upon my raw wound.

Psalm 147:3 – He heals the broken-hearted and bandages their wounds.

Learn to be gentle with yourself while in grief. Grieving takes a lot of energy. Simple tasks take much longer to accomplish, as if time is lived in slow motion. It is okay to allow oneself to mourn. It takes time to move through the pain of loss. Be patient in the process of grief.

It may feel like you are stuck in your mourning. Sometimes the journey of grief moves very slowly and sometimes you just need to rest. Resting does not mean that you are stuck, it just means that you are allowing reality to sink into your being. Breathe. Exhale and inhale. It takes time to work through the shattering sorrow.

Matthew 11:28 – Jesus said, "Come to me all of you who carry heavy burdens and I will give you rest."

Look to Jesus. He will breathe His peace upon you, assuring you of His deep love for you. He is the only One who can fill your broken soul with peace. He knows what to say and holds you close to His heart. Slowly, He will breathe life into your soul and help you function in this new reality.

Processing a loss includes reminiscing the good times, celebrating the delight of its presence. Hold those memories close. Find joy in them among your tears. When I realized that I did not have to let my daughter go, it gave me comfort.

In the midst of grief, there will be small spurts of joy. These joy-filled moments may bring guilt, for not being sad. Life becomes a twisting together of sorrow and joy.

Life is a tapestry of many threads. At the onset of the loss, grief is heavy. Loss causes the threads to be dark and deep in color. The thread of grief is not ugly, but precious. Grief brings depth of colour and pronounces vibrancy to the threads of joy. As healing unfolds, joy is allowed. The beauty of the tapestry is in its contrast of colours.

Since my daughter's death, I have a better understanding of grief and I know the reality of Jesus in the midst of deep sorrow. I can now speak with confidence that He understands, and holds us, when our heart breaks.

2 Corinthians 1:4 – He comforts us in all our troubles so that we can comfort others. When they are troubled, we will be able to give them the same comfort God has given us.

The following are some possible reasons why we cannot move forward in our grief journey:

- ANGER:

One of the possible stages of grief is anger. Two months after my daughter died, I woke one morning, angry at God. I had good reason to be angry; my Cherie had died and He had allowed it to happen. Losing her was so painful, and anger felt much better than feeling the deep sorrow. Anger protected me from feeling the pain of the heart-ripping separation from her. Reality was that she was gone and keeping the anger inhibited me from moving through my pain. So, I gave my anger to God, and asked Him to walk with me. He did, and still is. I went through my pain, facing it, processing what it looked like without my daughter. As I reflected and faced reality, with Jesus beside me, I was able to heal.

- ### SADNESS:

Sadness is a natural emotion when you have lost something precious. It is okay to be sad, but it is not okay for it to smother you. Though we have good reason to be sad, we do not have to be ruled by it. Just like anger, we can give our sadness to God, let Him carry it. Come to Jesus, He understands our sorrow.

Giving your sadness to God does not mean you are making light of the loss, rather, it is acknowledging your loss and allowing your soul to breathe, allowing it to be filled with joy. Give yourself permission to laugh and be happy. You are still alive. Though darkness has come into your life, determine to live your life with renewed purpose.

- ### GUILT:

As I journeyed through my own grief and listened to others speak of theirs, I was more and more convinced that guilt is very present in loss. We feel that we could have or should have done something different; it is our way of making sense of what happened. There are varying degrees of guilt but it seems to show its tormenting face amongst the sorrow.

Guilt can be a twist of both true and false accusations. For me, I felt guilty for not treating my daughter better, for not being aware of how serious her medical situation was, for not being there for her more than I was. It was a huge weight. Jesus showed me the difference between true and false guilt.

In reality, I was guilty of being impatient with her when she could not move faster. I was guilty for not spending more time with her, not being more attentive. That was real guilt. So, I confessed it to God and asked His forgiveness. Jesus died so that I do not have to carry guilt for the rest of my life. Guilt is heavy and restrictive. I chose to receive the gift of forgiveness and also forgive myself. Real guilt is convicting; it is based on truth.

Many times, after my daughter's death, I felt guilty when I brushed my teeth, realizing that I did not swab her dry mouth while she was in the hospital. It may sound trivial but it pierced my soul. I had to let this false guilt go. I was not aware of how serious her condition was, and the thought of swabbing her mouth did not enter my thoughts. I realized that I should not take on guilt for something that I did not know. I had to let it go. Try as I might, I could not make her life 'normal', so why would I feel guilty over something that was not possible? False guilt is condemning; it is not based on truth.

Ask God to help you discern what is true or false guilt. With true guilt, you ask for forgiveness from Jesus. He died for that guilt. Receive His forgiveness and forgive yourself. It will give you the freedom to move forward. With false guilt, you simply let it go. It never was yours to carry.

- ## WANTING TO STAY STUCK:
Staying in one's grief gives us permission not to move forward. It takes courage to proceed with life, moving onward. Jesus spoke to me in the midst of my grief, saying, "The future stands on the past, it doesn't dwell in it."

I understood that to mean that I need to rise out of my grief and not stay stuck in it. Just as a planted seed sprouts, shooting out of the soil to produce a stalk, so can I rise out of my sorrow. I grow out from my sorrow. The seed is what forms the new growth, my future. The seed is what gives

204

substance to what it becomes. I have gone through a dark valley and the darkness has brought another facet of understanding grief. I choose to move through it and into my new reality with its richness.

I can speak with absolute confidence that Jesus is beside me. He is present when experiencing joy, and with me in the midst of intense hardship. My belief in His trustworthiness is based on evidence that He is reliable, even when I do not understand His plan, and His timing. He has purpose in all things. There was a definite purpose in my daughter dying exactly when she did. I keep moving through my sorrow. I continue to face memories, with Jesus right beside me.

SUICIDE:

Suicide leaves a deep wounding of the soul. It pierces into the midst of one's being, ripping it apart. We try to make sense of it, by blaming someone, or we condemn ourselves for not preventing it.

I had a dear friend who committed suicide many years ago. It happened at the end of winter after the long seasonal darkness of my northern region. My friend, Lynn, lost all hope. Financially she struggled, her two grown children wanted nothing to do with her, her ex-husband was seeing another woman, her brother instilled fear in her because of his dangerous life style, and her body hurt intensely due to fibromyalgia. When we got together, we laughed, and her spirit lifted – temporarily. That particular winter, I did not visit Lynn as much, because I was busy helping my daughter with her newborn son.

One day, Lynn was found dead, overdosed on her medications. My heart was crushed, condemning myself for not spending more time with her. It was my fault.

I went to Jesus with my incredible guilt. It was so very heavy, suffocating. He spoke into my mind, "Irene, you have been close friends with her for five years. You have walked with her, laughed with her, and brought her joy. You made it possible for her to live these five years. You did your part. You are not guilty." His words brought a deep sense of peace within my soul. It was okay. It was Lynn's decision to take her life. I am not responsible for her choice.

Sometimes we are able to walk suicidal people through their intentions to end their life, but we do not have the ability to extinguish it. We do not hold that power and should not feel guilty. Hand that false guilt over to God. He does not hold you responsible for their choice. God understands their desperate, broken heart and He does not condemn them for their struggles. He was present when it happened; they were not alone when they took their life. He was there beside them, looking at them with His eyes of compassion. He gave them choice.

Come before God and let Him still your soul. Confess any real guilt and let go of the false guilt. Let Him hold you in your deep sorrow. You will be okay. Let Him breathe His life into your being.

Psalm 62:8 - O my people, trust in Him at all times. Pour out your heart to Him for God is our refuge.

JESUS SPEAKS INTO GRIEF:
- Roger's brother, Harold, was heavy into drugs and one day, he was found dead. It was heartbreaking. We went to Jesus with Roger's pain. Jesus told him that He was there with his brother, and that he had died quietly. Jesus had taken him home. Seven years before his death, Harold had given his heart to Jesus. From that day forward, Jesus had kept his heart safe. One day Roger will see him again. Those beautiful words of peace flooded Roger's heart.
- Belinda came into my office broken-hearted. Her wails were heard down the hall. She was shattered by the

agony of her dear cousin fatally overdosing. She had just met with him the past evening, and this morning he was dead. Her soul was overtaken with deep grief. I felt the Holy Spirit prompting me to enclose her in my firm embrace. That was what Jesus would have done. I held her for forty minutes as her body heaved and her trembling voice cried out in intense pain. Slowly her heart quietened, her soul became calm. She experienced the presence of Jesus holding her. He physically did it through me. I became His arms of love. Jesus' presence brought peace to her soul.

- Geraldine lost her best friend of ten years, due to a highway accident. She felt alone, scared, and empty, like nobody cared. She felt lost. When going back into the memory, she discovered that Jesus was present, right beside her. His tender arms wrapped around her, making her feel loved, accepted, and filled with joy. His Presence did not take the pain away, yet it soothed her soul and comforted her. She was not alone; Jesus was with her and He understood her pain.

- Ivan was an alcoholic father. His fifteen-year-old son begged him to stop drinking, but Ivan could not, would not. Two weeks later, Ivan was at his friend's house and received a phone call that his son had been in a serious accident. They rushed to the scene. The night air was filled with the piercing strobe lights of the police cars and ambulance. His son was no where in sight. Ivan finally discovered the body of his beloved son in the field. He wept in remorse, believing that it was his fault that his son had died. He was overwhelmed with guilt.

In an Inner Healing session, Jesus spoke to Ivan, telling him that his son's death was not his fault. Ivan gave God his guilt for drinking (real guilt), received God's forgiveness, and forgave himself. He let go of blaming himself for his son's death (false guilt). Jesus told Ivan that he had time to change. Hope birthed within his heart.

Those of us who have lost a loved one, long to connect with them. We miss them. A friend of mine asked me if it was okay to meet with a medium in order to contact her son, after he had died by suicide. God warns us not to go to a medium.

Leviticus 19:31 – Do not defile yourselves by turning to mediums or to those who consult the spirits of the dead. I am the Lord your God.

When you invite the supernatural to enter your grief, you give control to the one you seek. If you intentionally open yourself to spirits other than Jesus, you give Satan opportunity to deceive you into believing that you are hearing your loved one's voice, seeing that person. Satan is a liar, that is how he gets access into your thinking. Exposing your heart to the supernatural, other than the Holy Spirit, allows demonic forces to influence you.

Jesus understands your longing to be with the loved person who died. He knows about it. Go to the One who speaks truth. His truth sets you free to live in peace. Come to Jesus and allow Him to fill you with peace. Go to the One who understands your sorrow and allow Him to walk with you through your grief. Only Jesus is able to fill you with a deep peace. If you have gone to a medium to contact your deceased loved one, repent to God for going to a psychic instead of to Him.

PRAYER: for Cleansing
Dear Jesus. I am so sorry for going to a psychic/medium in order to have contact with my loved one who died. I wanted to contact them so badly, but now I realize that it was wrong. It has defiled my spirit and I renounce its hold on me. Please

cleanse my soul and remove any influence that this experience has had on me, in the name of Jesus. I receive your forgiveness. Thank you for dying for my sin, dear Jesus. I choose to trust you and I release my loved one into your hands. Fill me with your peace. I give my life to you. I pray this in Jesus' name, Amen.

I have spoken to numerous people who have told me they have sensed the presence of their deceased loved one. I too have experienced the presence of my daughter after her death. This is very different than going to a medium, for I was not intentionally trying to connect with her. It was God giving me the experience of my daughter, when He chose to do so. I do not know why or how it happened. I have no explanation. It happened out of nowhere, for no reason that I am aware of. All I know is that it happened, and it brought great warmth to my heart.

Jesus understands your sorrow, your grief. He was present in the midst of the loss. Invite Him into your pain. Allow His love to surround you. You are not alone. He holds you and speaks to you, soothes your anguished soul. "Peace, peace be unto you, my child. I love you and I am always with you in whatever happens, wherever you are."

PRAYER: for Peace
Oh Lord, I desperately want your peace. My heart is in anguish over (my loss). It aches and feels severely torn inside, like I will never be the same again. I ask you to hold me in my bottomless sorrow. Embrace my broken heart and breathe life into my being. Thank you for understanding. Thank you for being beside me. I put (my loss) into your hands. Fill me with your peace. I open my heart to You. I want to feel joy again. Touch my bleeding heart and heal my wounds. I give you my sadness; wipe my tears away. Surround me with your Presence. I receive your peace. Thank you for walking with me. Hold me, dear Jesus.

Even when I walk
through the darkest valley,
I will not be afraid,
for You are close beside me.
Your rod and Your staff protect me
and comfort me.
- Psalm 23:4

REFLECTIONS: Chapter 14 – Grieving with Jesus

1. What losses have your experienced?
2. How do you deal with your grief?
3. Grief is a journey.
   What keeps you moving through it?
4. Do you have any true or false guilt regarding your loss?
   Ask Jesus to show you the difference.
   Confess true guilt and receive Jesus' forgiveness.
   Forgive yourself.
   Release false guilt.
5. How can your future grow out of this grief?
6. Have you had to deal with suicide?
7. Why does God instruct us not to go to a medium or psychic?

Notes & Journaling:

PART 5

Experiencing the Delight of His Presence

We can stand tall
no matter what life brings,
for nothing can separate us
from the love of God.

Jesus is able to transform
the most devastating situation
into a glorious one.

Praise declares that
Jesus is trustworthy.

Experiencing Him
brings ultimate satisfaction
within the soul.

Chapter 15

Standing: More than Conquerors

There was a story about a donkey who fell into a well hole. Its urgent braying rose up from the pit, alerting the people of its fate. The villagers tried to rescue the donkey, but all their efforts were futile. They cried out to the wise man, but he too could not come up with a working solution. It became apparent that the donkey could not be rescued. He was doomed.

Seeing no way to save the animal, the villagers decided to fill the hole. Clumps of earth were thrown into the pit. The dirt landed on the donkey's back with a heavy thump. The creature's destiny was sealed: death was inevitable. But the donkey shook the dirt from his back and stomped it under his feet. With each spade of dirt, the donkey rose higher and higher. The dirt, intended to bury him, became his means of liberation.

We have all lived through traumatizing events that have tried to bury us. Overcome us. Overwhelm us. But we made it. Stand up – Jesus declares we are more than Conquerors.

Romans 8:37 – No, in all these things we are more than conquerors through Him who loved us. (NIV)

Victory is ours. His spoken word is truth, and the truth sets us free[161] – free from fear and all the taunting voices that mock us. We are no longer at the mercy of what is going on around us, we have confidence in the presence of Jesus. It is Christ's death on the cross, and His victory in rising from the dead,

---

[161] John 8:32

that crowns us as more than conquerors. This is why we are unshakeable, anchored securely in Him. Stand up. Take the prize. We are the winners.

Winning is:
- not about overpowering others.
- not about forcing others into submission.
- not about screaming in anger so someone will give in.

Conquering is not about domination; it is about submission to God. Winning comes from the inside; a 'knowing' that we are Victors, no matter what happens on the outside.

When Jesus was on trial, before He was nailed to the cross, a multitude of accusations were hurled at Him. They said He was a liar. A deceiver. A weakling. He spoke not a word to defend himself. He kept standing. He knew who He was, and knew His purpose. He stood before His Father, in submission to His will. Because of His death and resurrection, He conquered all the powers of evil, victoriously. He liberated our souls from Satan's grip – so we can stand strong and confidently. Jesus has already won the war of our souls. He bought us and redeemed us with the payment of His blood. We are conquerors, because Jesus conquered. Jesus is the Victor. He is our Champion.

Psalm 62:1-2 – I wait quietly before God, for my victory comes from Him. He alone is my Rock and my Salvation, my Fortress where I will never be shaken.

GIDEON'S STORY:
The book of Judges, Chapter 7, speaks of Gideon gathering an army of 30,000 men to fight the Midianites. God told him that his army had too many men. Too many men to conquer the enemy! Too many men to bring victory! God instructed Gideon to eliminate thousands of men from his army. There were still

too many. Eliminate more! Three hundred men were left, standing before Gideon. That was exactly right. Gideon believed that His God was trustworthy, even though logic laughed mockingly in his face. God knew these three hundred men were the perfect number. The number for victory, not defeat. And they did conquer their enemies – God's way.

Zechariah 4:6 – "It is not by force nor by strength, but by my Spirit," says the Lord of Heaven's Armies.

DANIEL'S STORY:
Daniel, from the Old Testament,[162] vowed to serve his God no matter the consequences. He and his two friends refused to bow down to the King's statue. They stood. They were not going to deny God, even if their lives were at stake. In a rage, the King ordered the furnace to be heated seven times hotter than usual, then Daniel and his friends were thrown into it. The men who flung them into the furnace died from the heat. But Daniel and his friends did not die. They strolled amid the chamber, walking, and talking. They were alive, not overcome. When they were released, they did not even smell like smoke.

Isaiah 43:2-3 – When you go through deep waters, I will be with you. When you go through rivers of difficulty, you will not drown. When you walk through the fire of oppression, you will not be burned up; the flames will not consume you. For I am the Lord, your God, the Holy One of Israel, your Saviour.

JUDEAN ARMY'S STORY:
The Judean army was overwhelmed with fear of warring against three armies at one time. God gave one man a message: "They will not have to fight; God will battle for

---

[162] Daniel 3

217

them." Their hearts believed it. They knew that God was reliable.

Early the next morning, they stood up and began to march. The King assigned singers to walk ahead of the army. They sang with gusto. They were filled with joy. They knew they were winners before the battle had even begun. They praised God. A huge chorus of adoration was lifted to their God. II Chronicles 20:22 states that at the very moment the people began to praise God, the three enemy armies began to fight amongst themselves. They fatally struck their enemies, savagely annihilating each other.

When King Jehoshaphat and his army reached the lookout point, they observed dead bodies as far as their eyes could see. Not a single enemy soldier had escaped. God had fought the battle for them. They were victorious, without having to fight.

Isaiah 12:2-5 – See, God has come to save me. I will trust in Him and not be afraid. The Lord God is my strength and my song, He has given me victory. With joy you will drink deeply from the fountain of salvation! Thank the Lord! Praise His name! Tell the nations what He has done. Let them know how mighty He is! Sing to the Lord, for He has done wonderful things. Make known His praise around the world.

Praise is a powerful weapon. Praise is a confident knowing that our God is trustworthy.
- It is not dependent on our circumstances.
- It is based on who God is.

We stand – knowing that God, our Creator, is trustworthy. Nothing can change who He is.
- God has been faithful in the past.
- He is unchanging today.

- He will be trustworthy throughout all our tomorrows.

Praise is possible because God is loving, compassionate, kind, forgiving, and patient. God does not change in character. He is trustworthy no matter what our eyes see or our hearts feel. God's Word is truth. Our praise overtakes the powers of darkness. Praise crowns us as more than conquerors.

Psalm 34:1 – I will praise the Lord at all times. I will constantly speak His praises. I will boast only in the Lord; let all who are helpless take heart. Come, let us tell of the Lord's greatness; let us exalt His name together.

PAUL'S AND SILAS' STORY:

Paul and Silas were beaten with wooden rods, then thrown into jail. Their feet were clamped in stocks. Acts 16:25 states that, around midnight, they began singing praises to God. Their melodies of worship floated through the darkness of night. It was tender, yet powerful. They sang of God's love and faithfulness. The presence of Jesus permeated the air. Paul's and Silas' hearts were bursting in adoration of the One who had died for them, then rose from the dead. How they loved Jesus. Though their bodies held marks of being beaten, their hearts were free in that putrid jail.

Then the earth shook. The prison doors flew open. Their chains were released. They stood – free.

Psalm 103:1-2 – Let all that I am praise the Lord; with my whole heart, I will praise His holy name. Let all that I am praise the Lord; may I never forget the good things He does for me.

MAMA LUCY'S STORY:

Mama Lucy grew up in an abusive home; it was crushing and overwhelmingly difficult. That little girl vowed before God to one day, help a child who was suffering hardship. At age twenty, when Lucy saw a street boy, she remembered her promise to God, and invited the boy to stay with her. She wanted to take care of him. Over the following days, nine more joined him in her one-bedroom apartment. In her crowded state, she moved them to her home region and the number grew to seventy children. Some days, there were potatoes or cabbage to eat; other days, no food. She kept calling upon God; He heard her.

This big family smiled and laughed together. They knew God had not abandoned them; He was their Father. Today, Mama Lucy has a large family of several hundred children, some graduated from universities and colleges, some starting their own families. Against all odds, this single woman stood triumphant, overcoming fear and every obstacle. Not only did she have a future, so did her precious children. Their hearts were radiant, praising God.

Jeremiah 29:11 – "For I know the plans I have for you," says the Lord, "They are plans for good and not for disaster, to give you a future and a hope."

NICK VUJICIC'S STORY:

Nick struggled emotionally throughout his childhood and into young adulthood. For what purpose was he born – without arms or legs? Being the target for school bullies, Nick became severely depressed and contemplated suicide. One day, he read an article about a severely disabled man. That story inspired Nick to discover how to accomplish the tasks of limbed people – to write, type, play, and shave. He discovered his purpose – inspiring others to make their lives and world better.

Today, he is married and has four children. As an evangelist, he proclaims that, with courage and faith in God, any adversity can be overcome. His organization, 'Life without

Limbs', as well as his book, 'Life Without Limits', has changed millions of lives.

Nick Vujicic stated:
- "If you can't get a miracle, become one."[163]
- "Do not give up because you do not know what's around the corner."[164]
- "If God can use a man without arms and legs to be His hands and feet, then He will certainly use any willing heart!"[165]

2 Corinthians 12:8-9 – Each time He said, "My grace is all you need. My power works best in weakness." So now I am glad to boast about my weaknesses, so that the power of Christ can work through me.

JONI ERICKSON TADA'S STORY:
At age 16, Joni became paralyzed from her shoulders down, as a result of a diving accident. As a teenager and young adult, she struggled with her faith in God, beseeching God to miraculously heal her. But God had other plans for Joni, a different kind of miracle, that would inspire many throughout the world.

Today, Joni is a powerful speaker regarding suffering and the endearment of her precious God, after more than fifty years in a wheelchair. Through her ministry, 'Joni and Friends', she has brought hope and fulfilment to thousands of people with disabilities. She has written books, painted beautiful art with her mouth, recorded albums of her singing, and has been

---

[163] Nick Vujicic Quotes (Author of *Life Without Limits*),
https://www.goodreads.com/author/quotes/3395320.
[164] Nick Vujicic quotes that will inspire you achieve excellence, yourselfquotes.com
[165] Nick Vujicic, TFP, thefamouspeople.com

married for over thirty years. Joni has had cancer twice, and is in constant pain in recent years, yet her faith in Her Lord Jesus stands confidentially, anchored in His Presence and love for her.

Joni Erickson Tada stated:
- "He has chosen not to heal me, but to hold me. The more intense the pain, the closer His embrace."[166]
- "I'd rather be in this wheelchair knowing God than on my feet without Him."[167]

Romans 5:3-5 – We can rejoice, too, when we run into problems and trials, for we know that they help us develop endurance. And endurance develops strength of character, and character strengthens our confident hope of salvation. And this hope will not lead to disappointment. For we know how dearly God loves us because He has given us the Holy Spirit to fill our hearts with His love.

CORNELIA A. J. "CORRIE" TEN BOOM'S STORY:

The miracle of forgiveness is very real to Corrie ten Boom. Her family helped many Jews escape the Gestapo's Holocaust, during World War II, by hiding them in their home. In 1944, they were reported by a man, arrested, and sent to experience the horrors of Ravensbruck concentration camp.

When Corrie was released, she travelled for three decades, telling people of her story and the need to forgive. After one of her meetings, she was greeted by a man whom she recognized as one of the most vicious guards at

---

[166] Joni Erickson Tada (2010). *A Place of Healing: Wrestling with the Mysteries of Suffering, Pain, and God's Sovereignty*, p.35, David C Cook.
[167] Joni Erickson Tada Quotes, azquotes.com

Ravensbruck. He extended his hand to her, and declared that God had forgiven him of his cruel actions.

Excerpt from *7 Women: and the Secret of their Greatness*:[168]

'Corrie remembered that forgiveness is an act of will – not an emotion. "Jesus, help me!" she prayed. "I can lift my hand. I can do that much. You supply the feeling." Corrie thrust out her hand. And as she did, an incredible thing took place:

> The current started in my shoulder, raced down my arm, sprang into our joined hands. And then this healing warmth seemed to flood my whole being, bringing tears to my eyes. "I forgive you, brother!" I cried. "With all my heart." For a long moment we grasped each others' hands, the former guard, and the former prisoner. I had never known God's love so intensely as I did then. But even so, I realized it was not my love. I had tried, and did not have the power. It was the power of the Holy Spirit.'[169]

Philippians 4:13 – I can do everything through Christ, who gives me strength.

We are more than conquerors over:

CIRCUMSTANCES - We stand confidently in the midst of hardship.

2 Corinthians 4:8-9 – We are pressed on every side by troubles, but we are not crushed. We are perplexed, but not driven to despair. We are hunted down, but never abandoned by God. We get knocked down but we are not destroyed.

---

[168] Eric Metaxas, *7 Women: and the Secret of their Greatness*, copyright Thomas Nelson

[169] Eric Metaxas, *The Test of Forgiveness: Corrie ten Boom*, July 24, 2019, faithgateway.com

- **WORRIES** - Our confidence in Him overrules panic and anxiety.

Philippians 4:6-7: Do not worry about anything: instead, pray about everything. Tell God what you need, and thank Him for all He has done. Then you will experience God's peace, which exceeds anything we can understand. His peace will guard your hearts and minds as you live in Christ Jesus.

- **FEAR** - Peace invades and overtakes fear.

2 Corinthians 1:8-10 – We were crushed and overwhelmed beyond our ability to endure, and we thought we would never live through it. In fact, we expected to die. As a result, we stopped relying on ourselves and learned to rely only on God, who raises the dead. And He did rescue us from mortal danger; and He will rescue us again. We have placed our confidence in Him and He will continue to rescue us.

SATAN'S ATTACKS - We have victory over opposing supernatural forces.

Ephesians 6:10, 13-14 - Be strong in the Lord and in His mighty power. . . Put on every piece of God's armour so you will be able to resist the enemy in the time of evil. Then after the battle you will still be standing firm. Stand your ground . . .

THE POWERS OF HELL - The love of God within us defeats the powers of hell itself.

Romans 8:38-39 – And I am convinced that nothing can ever separate us from God's love. Neither death nor life, neither angels nor demons, neither our fears for today nor our worries about tomorrow - not even the powers of hell can separate us from God's love. No power in the sky above or in the earth below – indeed, nothing in all creation will ever be able to separate us from the love of God that is revealed in Christ Jesus our Lord.

Our confidence in Jesus makes us extraordinarily triumphant:
- The sting of death cannot pierce our soul;
  death brings the fulfilment of hope.
- Our dreams are not crushed;
  they are transformed.
- The trials of life cannot overpower us;
  they build our faith.
- Brokenness becomes a spectacular masterpiece,
  an iridescent display of God's powerful love.

There is a story regarding the origin of stained-glass windows. During the war, a bomb was dropped on a German town. All the windows of their little cathedral shattered. Their sacred place of refuge was devastated. But piece by piece, the broken shards were soldered together. Instead of gaping window holes, the sunlight radiated through beautiful stained-glass windows. Magnificent masterpieces heralded the presence of God Himself. Hope was emitted from its beauty; its glow radiated God's love to mankind.

As I reflect over the years of my life, I see a brilliant demonstration of God's love and His faithfulness throughout my life, even during the deep dark valley of death, when my daughter died. When it was the darkest, Jesus' Presence was the most spectacular.

Peace is possible in the midst of a tremendous storm. Jesus is present, right beside us. He holds us. Breathes life into our being. No matter how ferocious the hurricane, how powerful the tsunami, how violent the crashing waves, we take refuge in His presence – and peace prevails. His tender whisperings quiet our souls. And we fly as eagles. We soar above the storms of the night. We are safe.

We turn to Jesus, our Champion, when we are:
- helpless, crying out in fear and anxiety.
- threatened to be overcome by our guilt and shame.
- mocked by voices of condemnation.
- taken captive by our deep woundedness.
- unable to laugh because we are full of anger.
- cannot forgive those who have hurt us deeply.
- hesitate to forgive ourselves.

When we look into the tender eyes of Jesus. He fills us with:
- confident hope of standing tall.
- miraculous healing of our soul, mind, and body.
- power to forgive.
- inner peace.
- defined purpose.
- incredible worth.
- indescribable love.
- abundant life.

Romans 8:31-32 - If God is for us, who can ever be against us? Since He did not spare even His own Son but gave Him up for us all, won't He also give us everything else?

We are more than conquerors – not by outwitting, maneuvering, tricking, deceiving, and manipulating. It is more than our human ability; it goes beyond positive thinking. We are more than conquerors because Jesus is THE Champion. He is our Leader, and we stand, choosing to follow Him. We are filled with His power and strength. We stand confidently. All glory to Jesus; glory to His name.

With Jesus at our side, with Him directing our life, because He loves us and fills our hearts with His love, we stand tall. We are more than conquerors.

- We are able to live
  – vibrantly.
- We become the people whom He has created us to be
  – perfectly.
- Because we receive His love, we can love others
  – wholeheartedly.
- We have purpose
  – to know Him, receive Him and live in Him.

The incredible Presence of Jesus is:
- exciting.
- passionate.
- exuberant living.
- beyond all imagination or highest dreams.

Jesus is with us – always has been, always will be
                    – forever and ever.

Now all glory to God, who is able,
through His mighty power at work within us,
to accomplish infinitely more
than we might ask or think.
Glory to Him in the church
and in Christ Jesus
through all generations forever and ever!
Amen and AMEN
- Ephesians 3:20-21

REFLECTIONS: Chapter 15 – More Than Conquerors

1. What are things in life that you will NOT be buried under?
2. How can submission to God make you more than a conqueror?
3. How is it possible to praise God in devastating circumstances?
4. What is your story of brokenness, transforming into an amazing masterpiece?

Notes & Journaling:

Chapter 16

Basking in His Presence

I LOVE JESUS. I ADORE HIM.

Jesus sits beside me and I look into His eyes. I know that He loves me for His eyes portray His delight.

He created me. Tenderly He formed me in my mother's womb. His masterpiece. He watched me as I was birthed. He breathed life into my lungs.

I grew into a teenager and became aware of His Presence. I began to recognize His voice. It was kind, always speaking truth to me.

As life unfolded, challenges and trials threatened to overtake me. I went to Him. I needed Him. He did not push me away when I struggled and failed. Instead, He died for me.

He paid the price of my guilt with His blood. He released me from having to earn my salvation. He encouraged me to cling to Him. And I did. He wiped away my tears, not forever, but for that moment. I trusted in His love, even when life's situations did not make sense. His peace flooded over my woundedness. His tender love touched the depth of my soul, invading the darkness, filling it with unexplainable joy.

Jesus is alive! I know He is, because He lives within my heart. I have no need to worry, no need to fear. He lifts me up and laughs with me, reassures me that He is with me.

He loved me - with His life.
Marked me - with His Spirit.
Chose me - as His own.
He is my Shepherd.

Psalm 23:
The Lord is my Shepherd; I have all I need.
He lets me rest in green meadows;
He leads me beside peaceful streams.
He renews my strength.
He guides me along right paths,
bringing honour to His name.
Even when I walk through the darkest valley,
I will not be afraid, for you are close beside me.
Your rod and your staff protect and comfort me.
You prepare a feast for me in the presence of my enemies.
You honour me by anointing my head with oil.
My cup overflows with blessings.
Surely your goodness and unfailing love will pursue me
all the days of my life,
and I will live in the house of the Lord forever.

One day, I will see Jesus face to face. One day, I will bow and worship Him at His feet. His joy will embrace me, delight in me. And I will be with Him - forever.

I invite you to come with me.
Come into His presence today.
He knows your name. Come.
He loves you deeply.
Open your heart and let Him in.

PRAYER: Receiving Jesus into your life.

Dear Father in Heaven. Thank you so much for sending your Son, Jesus, to this earth. Thank you, Jesus, for dying for my guilt so that I don't have to carry it anymore. I'm sorry for all the wrong things I've done in my life. Cleanse my heart of my guilt, and wash me clean. I receive your forgiveness as a gift from You.

Thank you for being with me, all the time. You know everything about me, and You love me deeply. I choose to trust You with my life and I ask You to open my life's pathway before me. I submit my will to You and choose to follow You. Fill my heart with your love; I open it to receive You. I love You, oh Lord. Fill me with your Holy Spirit. I receive your peace.

In the name of Jesus, Amen.

To all who believed in Him and accepted Him,
He gave the right to become the children of God.
– John 1:12

Psalm 18:1-2

I love you, Lord;
You are my strength.
The Lord is my Rock, my Fortress,
and my Saviour;
my God is my Rock,
in whom I find protection.
He is my Shield,
the power that saves me,
and my place of safety.

Oh, the Incredible
Presence of Jesus!

EPILOGUE

Healing within one's self is not easy. Dealing with lie-based childhood pain is emotionally exhausting. Do not give up. Keep going. If you fall into a cactus, would you not pull out the needles from your flesh? Of course, you would! Just so, keep owning your pain within the memory, let Jesus speak His truth, until the memory is entirely peaceful. It is possible.

Go back to the chapters which address how to deal with your pain. Ask Jesus to guide you and open the way for you. He knows the way. Trust Him. It is His truth that will set you free.

Healing takes time. The process of healing is dependent on several variables – the depth of the wound, the layers of protection around the wound, how willing you are in owning your pain, the presence of anger, willingness to receive forgiveness and forgive, and openness in receiving truth from Jesus. As you learn to trust Jesus, the fear dissipates.

Know that Jesus is already there in your pain-filled memory; you are not alone. His Presence will give you strength to face your pain. Be encouraged – God hears your heart's pleas; Jesus is right beside you and He understands. He is the Healer.

The Lord bless you, and keep you;

The Lord make His face shine on you,

and be gracious to you;

the Lord lift up His countenance on you,

– and give you peace.

– Numbers 6:24-26

Made in the USA
Monee, IL
12 August 2020

37896667R00138